The Sculpture Business

Documents from the Archive

Centre for the Study of Sculpture

HENRY MOORE INSTITUTE

Eric Gill at work on 'St Joan'
(Joan of Arc), *c.* early 1930s
245 × 193 mm
John Hoskin at work
c. early 1960s. 201 × 255 mm

Penelope Curtis

Introduction

An archive tells a story. It is a story which fills many of the gaps left by conventional histories of sculpture and by museum displays. The story in this book is only one story; there are endless permutations and possibilities.

This book gives a taste of the different ways of reading an archive, while at the same time taking us on an introductory journey through the sculptor's career, from the beginning to the end. It does not tell any one sculptor's story, nor does it lead us from the end of the 18th century to the end of the 20th. Instead it is much more mixed, partly to show how the elements are much the same – that any sculptor's career depends on training, contacts, business skills, clients, sales, exhibitions and profile – and that you only have to rearrange these elements, with slightly different emphasis, to produce any individual example.

The Sculpture Business

Sculptors are made, not born. They make themselves, and they are made
The career of every artist is a combination of the personal and the public; a combination of innate curiosity and talent with the opportunities available at a given historical moment. If this is true of any artist, it is particularly true of sculptors, whose work depends so much more on public recognition because of the greater costs and labour which are usually involved.

Sculpture is an expensive business
Setting up a sculpture workshop is relatively expensive. A sculptor needs to be fairly confident of the likelihood of future interest before making the necessary capital investment. Many sculptors have given up, or have been bankrupted, by the expense of maintaining a workshop and a workforce, and of having their works cast or fabricated. If something should go wrong – if a commission is turned down – the sculptor may have been involved in considerable expense, over a long period of time, from which there will be little chance of recuperating any costs.

Sculptors need to be able to balance costs, income against expenditure
Sculpture has often been a precarious business, and relatively fewer sculptors than painters have been successful in their careers. When a sculptor did succeed in operating a good business, with an eye on the need for a profit margin, they could corner the market and do extremely well. Henry Moore is the outstanding example of this possibility. In Moore's case, demand often outstripped supply, whereas many sculptors spend much of their time chasing possible leads; somewhere or someone to take their work.

Sculpture is all around us, visible or invisible
Sculpture has often suffered in comparison to painting because it costs more to make and is either more difficult, or impossible, to transport. In an age when exhibitions are the normal way in which we experience art, there is less opportunity to see sculpture than there is painting. Although the 20th century has seen a different way of making sculpture, developed specifically for the exhibition space, much of what had gone before was designed for a permanent position in a church, on a building, in a garden, in a graveyard, or on the street. Works such as these can rarely be moved for exhibitions, so we encounter them more rarely. We have to look out for them, and we have to look for them in different kinds of spaces.

Sculpture's Public Place

In recent times sculptors have been successful in establishing sculpture as a gallery art, just as much as painting. By removing sculpture from the street, from the functional or commemorative role it traditionally had, sculpture has been put alongside painting as an art for looking, judged on its own terms, and as a personal statement. However, sculptors in the 18th and 19th centuries, and still in the first half of the 20th century, were trained to think of sculpture's public position as being one of honour.

Documents from the archive

Our archive tells a particular version of a story. But though that story may be common enough, it is not well known.

Viewers rarely see behind the scenes of the sculpture business, or even 'think' behind the scenes. The archive represents the unfinished business that never saw the light of day, the preparations which lie behind a public monument, a commission, or an exhibition. It preserves things which were made, but which no longer exist.

Paperwork

Because of sculpture's public role, there are more documents involved. An archive devoted to sculpture can represent all the paperwork that comes with working with clients, committees and architects.

Records of the vanished

Sculpture is in some ways more vulnerable than other arts. If a building is demolished, if a politician falls from favour, or if sculpture is exposed to the elements or to vandalism, the only record might be in the archive, in the sculptor's drawings or in documentary photographs.

The dream or the doodle

Sculpture is vulnerable in other ways, even before it exists. A archive can preserve early ideas, or working sketches which never came to fruition. Sometimes sculptors had grandiose ideas for public monuments which could never have seen the light of the day, but the archive can preserve their fantasy. Other drawings are more modest, and may simply represent different solutions to one problem. Other plans and sketches may chart the whole process of working through from initial ideas, to blue-prints and models, but without the artist ever having secured the final vote of confidence in the project.

Finding the key

The archive can be opened up with a variety of different 'keys' cutting across the study of individual artists as isolated units. One could trawl the archive to tell the story of the public monument, the story of the client, the story of how sculpture has been exhibited. Of sculpture as something that is commercial, or as something that is deeply private. Though we have some holdings which document one sculptor's career in some detail, we have more holdings which, put together, clarify and exemplify the practice of sculpture in 20th-century Britain. Some of the most rewarding work to be done therefore is to use the archive like a sculpture collection and to select from it different exhibits, from different dates and different artists, tracking one phenomenon and its changing nature.

This book is one example of the approach, but acts primarily as a simple introduction to the life of the sculptor in its varied forms. Each of the pages of illustrations is designed to act as a sort of window onto something typical and important within the practice. There are almost always more examples to find, and the interested reader is invited to follow up any leads. University lecturers and college tutors would also be able to use this book as an example of the kind of material, and the kind of stories, which can be found in this archive. Groups can be taught using a pre-selected group of material. The archive is a teaching resource, and is growing as a collection of 'examples' or 'case studies'. Put together in an intelligent way, these case studies become more instructive and revealing of shifts and changes which might otherwise be invisible.

The Archive of the Centre for the Study of Sculpture

The particular story held within almost any archive is a combination of chance and design. Some items were purchased, others donated; some sculptors were sought out, other holdings came to us through mutual contacts or recommendations. In our case some people have made their way to the Centre for the Study of Sculpture because its name denotes its specialism, or because of the name and reputation of Henry Moore.

Henry Moore studied in Leeds, and was always grateful for the quality of the art education he received in this city. Before his death he returned to repay his debt, and through his Foundation invested in the City Art Gallery so as to bring together new galleries for the display of sculpture, and a Centre for further study by means of books and archival material. This initiative began in a relatively small way, within the City Art Gallery, in 1982. Since then the Henry Moore Foundation has only strengthened its commitment to Leeds, and to Moore's wish to make Leeds a place where sculpture could be studied. Whereas the Foundation's base – in Moore's home in Hertfordshire – is devoted exclusively to Moore and is indeed a perfect example of an archive in itself – the collections here are much broader in their range, and by no means focused on Moore.

Nevertheless, if the Henry Moore Foundation is effectively the Moore archive, the collections here might be seen as providing the background to Moore. Though the library reflects his diverse interests in sculpture of many periods and from many places, the collections can more properly be seen as representing the world in which Moore operated, within British sculpture of the 20th century, in its greater diversity. Though Moore represents one trajectory though that world, from the 1920s to the 1980s, many other kinds of sculpture and sculptors existed around him. While the sculpture collections can show Moore's better-known colleagues, like Hepworth, Underwood or Lambert, it is the archive which must aim to document the broader picture of British sculpture of that time. Whether or not we are interested in Moore, we cannot fail to understand him the better by knowing what else was happening at the same time. Because this activity was less famous, or was happening on the city street rather than in the art gallery, it is now only available through the archive.

The Henry Moore Foundation added to, both literally and metaphorically, what was already a strong municipal base for 20th century art. The Henry Moore Institute, opened in 1993, was deliberately sited alongside Leeds City Art Gallery. It is a specialist Institute, additional and complementary to a broad-based municipal collection. Because the strength of Leeds' sculpture collections lies in the 20th century, it makes sense for the collections of library and archive material to build on this, picking up connections with the artists already represented in the collection, or seeking to fill some of the areas which it cannot represent.

The Foundation was never concerned to build up its own collection, but instead to add value and depth to what was already at Leeds. It has made this possible by providing funds for the acquisition of archival material, which may, from time to time also include models and maquettes. By integrating the archive into the library, within the premises of the Institute, and by financing our recent appointment of an archivist, the Foundation has shown that it sees the archive as an integral part of our activities. This is demonstrated practically in terms of the working relationships negotiated and maintained by the curators of the different parts of the Centre's collection, who need to deal with the ambiguous status of some of the material we acquire, and its sometimes almost arbitrary allocation to the Archive, the Library's general or Special Collections, or to the sculpture collections. The increasingly fluid nature of modern sculpture, and of our understanding of its manifestations and need for documentation, demands that these collections interleave and interpenetrate on the most flexible of terms.

Representing sculpture properly and fully is complex, and thus involves a number of different kinds of collections. Nevertheless, those collections have to speak to each other, not least because of these grey areas which open up as soon as one starts to define them. We aim to represent the links between sculptures, models and maquettes, drawings, prints and sketches, documents and photographs, books and videos, invitation cards, press releases and reviews. All of these are necessary for an understanding of sculpture, particularly when it is site specific (as it has been in the past, and is again now, in a different way). And if we aim to represent sculpture across its different manifestations, and through the range of forms of its production, so we would like to represent a diverse range of its practitioners.

At present the archive is weighted by a few particularly voluminous holdings, and particularly that of the Thornycroft family, and Jacob Epstein. Thereafter we have important holdings of material relating to Frampton, Bradshaw, Wright and Peri, followed by Gill, Gilbert, Cawthra, Ledward and Armstead. (For details of all these sculptors, and the holdings, see the listing at the back.) It is clear then that our papers are British, and best represent the first half of the 20th century. The later 19th century is also represented in some considerable depth. We should now seek to represent more fully practice after 1960, and to bring more woman practitioners into the holdings. This book offers a reasonable survey of the sculpture business from the 1850s to the 1950s, but neither does justice to the work of the avant-garde, nor, and more particularly, to the changing nature of sculpture over the last two or three decades. Though such work is represented in the collections of sculptures, and of works on paper, as well as in the library, we need to work harder to bring its accessory material into the archive.

The Archive only becomes more vital as the definition of sculpture itself becomes not only more difficult, but also increasingly contentious. It is the archive which can deal with the oral, the conceptual, the pre-life or the posterity. It can record the temporary, the context, the reception. On the one hand sculpture is currently seen as only too healthy; over-ready to embrace a whole range of kindred spirits. Some sculptors question the over-expansion of what was previously a more narrowly defined field. Others enthusiastically welcome the inclusion of other disciplines – film and installation, text and architecture, sound and time – into sculpture's field. And others again work from an opposing position, maintaining that it is no longer possible to make the sculptural object and that sculpture itself is now effectively meaningless. Both positions have their reasons for being. Fortunately the archive need declare itself for neither, but can operate between the two, and, in its modest way, negotiate some of that difficult terrain which makes being involved in sculpture, and in archives, so interestingly full of potential.

The business of sculpture has changed considerably over the last two centuries, but even now there is still a formal framework in place for the training, examination and assessment of sculptors, who then go on to promote their careers by means of exhibitions, sales and public commissions. The material held in the archive reveals not only the continuities over the last two hundred years, but also the sheer amount of paper associated with the business-side of sculpture. The paperwork that was used and saved by individuals, as a necessary part of their working life, is what we can now use to understand the nature of the professional practice of sculpture. The following pages take us on a tour through the sculptor's life, with selected documents throwing light on its different stages.

In the 18th and 19th centuries, as these two indentures of apprenticeship show, one could learn to be a sculptor by working as an assistant within the established practice of a more senior figure. Although the apprenticeship system no longer has a formal role to play in training young sculptors, there is still a tradition, and particularly in sculpture, of more successful artists taking on their younger colleagues to help them with some of the more routine or more arduous work. Henry Moore, who had such a flourishing business in post-war Britain, was particularly well placed to take on a number of helpers who later went on to make a name for themselves independently.

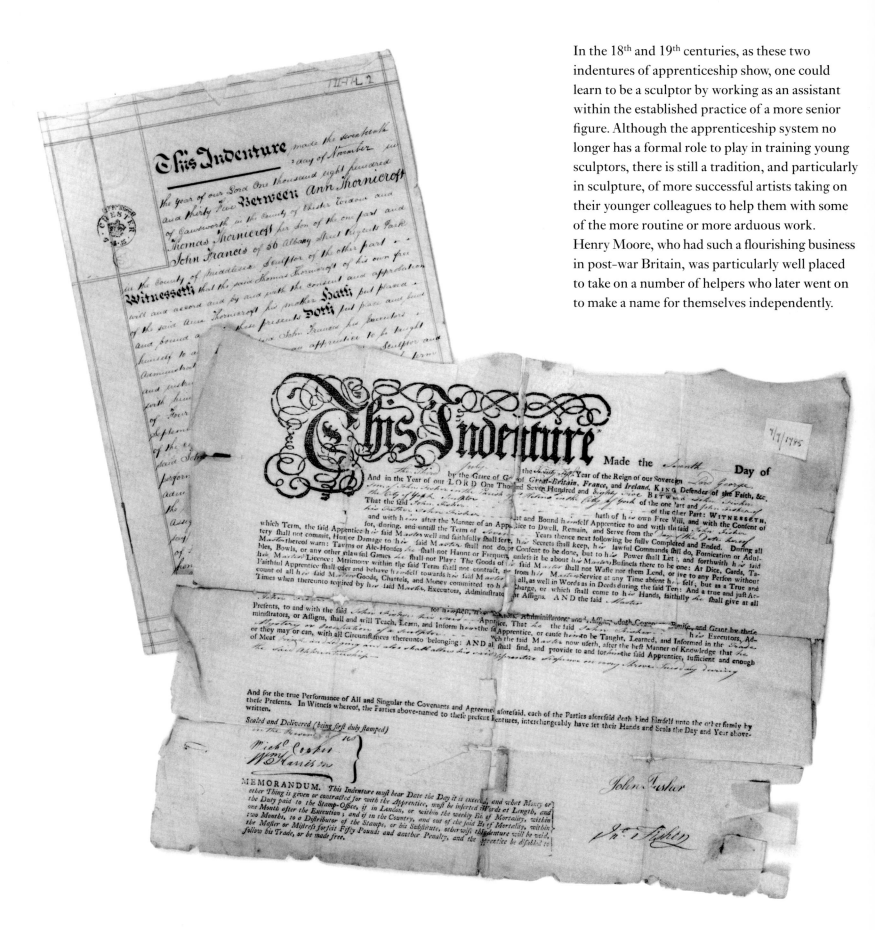

Indenture of apprenticeship between Ann Thornycroft and **Thomas Thornycroft**, her son, of the one part and John Francis 56 Albany Street Regents Park in the county of Middlesex sculptor of the other part, 1835. 317 × 396 mm. Indenture between **John Fisher**, son of John Fisher in the Parish of St Helena in the City of York of the one part and John Fisher of the city of York sculptor of the other part, 1785. 373 × 320 mm

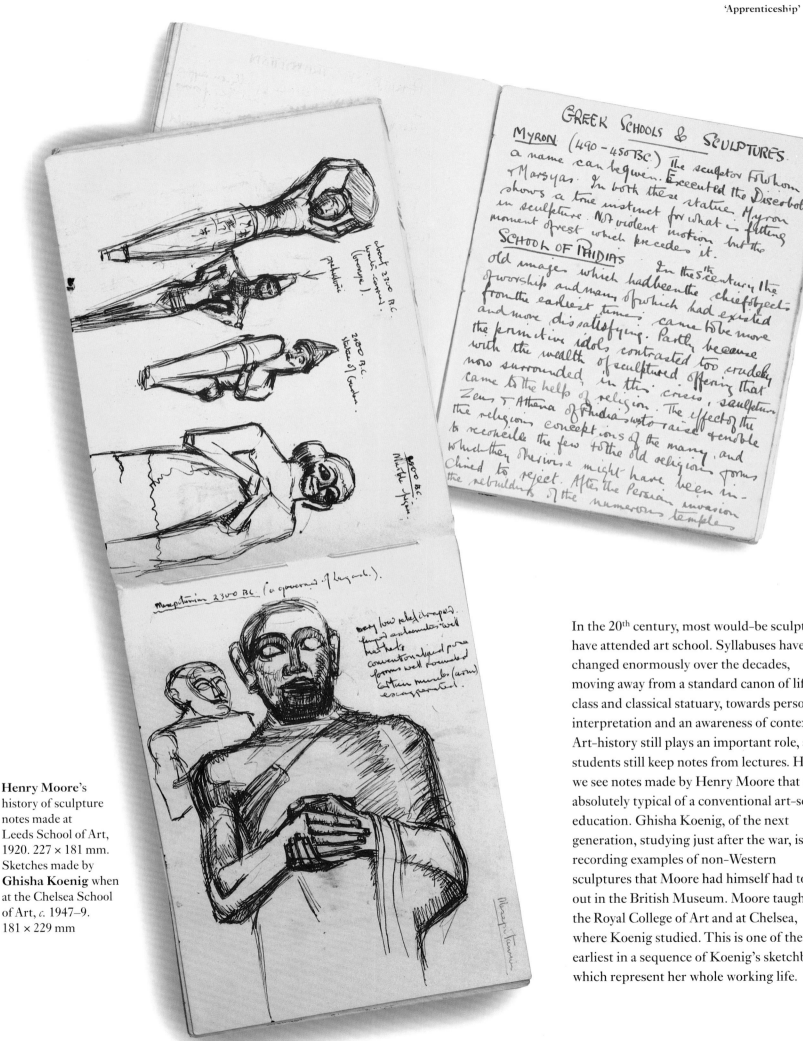

Henry Moore's history of sculpture notes made at Leeds School of Art, 1920. 227 × 181 mm. Sketches made by **Ghisha Koenig** when at the Chelsea School of Art, *c.* 1947–9. 181 × 229 mm

In the 20th century, most would–be sculptors have attended art school. Syllabuses have changed enormously over the decades, moving away from a standard canon of life class and classical statuary, towards personal interpretation and an awareness of context. Art-history still plays an important role, and students still keep notes from lectures. Here we see notes made by Henry Moore that are absolutely typical of a conventional art-school education. Ghisha Koenig, of the next generation, studying just after the war, is recording examples of non-Western sculptures that Moore had himself had to seek out in the British Museum. Moore taught at the Royal College of Art and at Chelsea, where Koenig studied. This is one of the earliest in a sequence of Koenig's sketchbooks which represent her whole working life.

Museum pass admitting Mr Brockedon, Englishman, to the Capitoline musem, signed by **Antonio Canova**, 1821. 211 × 194 mm

Visiting galleries, historic sites, and private collections is an important part of artistic education. It is now much more possible for a larger number of students, whereas in the 18th and earlier 19th centuries such opportunities were only available to the privileged few, and often took place as part of the aristocratic Grand Tour of Italy and Greece. This pass, allowing the bearer access to the Capitoline Collections, and signed by the great sculptor Canova, reminds us of how the tradition has changed in the succeeding generations.

Page one and four of a letter from **Henry Moore** to Jocelyn Horner with imagined views of Norway, *c.* 1923. First page of a letter by Henry Moore to Jocelyn Horner, *c.* 1923. 151 × 113 mm & 203 × 161 mm

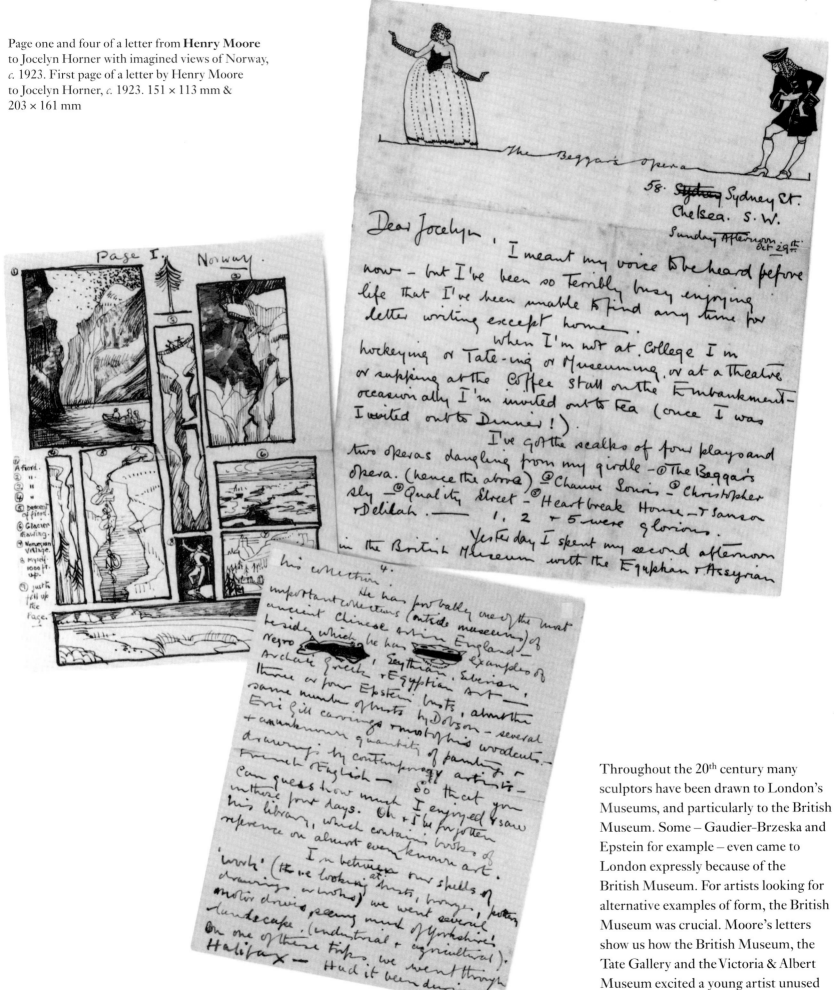

Throughout the 20th century many sculptors have been drawn to London's Museums, and particularly to the British Museum. Some – Gaudier-Brzeska and Epstein for example – even came to London expressly because of the British Museum. For artists looking for alternative examples of form, the British Museum was crucial. Moore's letters show us how the British Museum, the Tate Gallery and the Victoria & Albert Museum excited a young artist unused to such metropolitan delights.

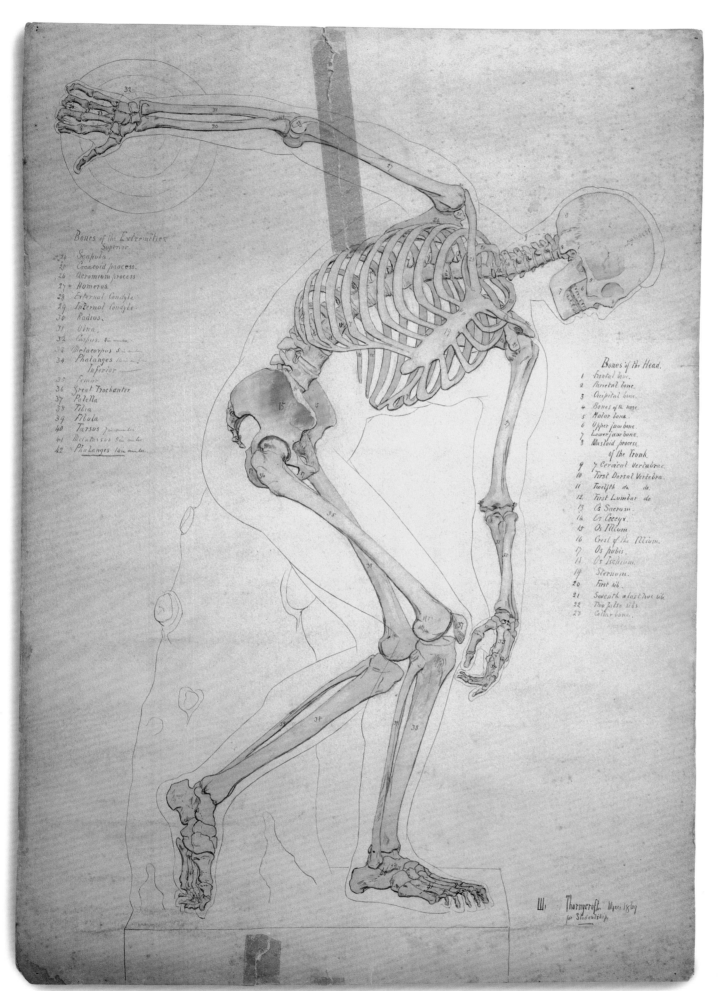

Bones of the Extremities
Superior
24 Scapula.
25 Coracoid process.
26 Acromium process.
27 Homerus.
28 External Condyle.
29 Internal Condyle.
30 Radius.
31 Ulna.
32 Carpus.
33 Metacarpus.
34 Phalanges.
Inferior
35 Femur.
36 Great Trochanter.
37 Patella.
38 Tibia.
39 Fibula.
40 Tarsus.
41 Metatarsus.
42 Phalanges.

Bones of the Head.
1 Frontal bone.
2 Parietal bone.
3 Occipital bone.
4 Bones of the nose.
5 Malar bone.
6 Upper jaw bone.
7 Lower jaw bone.
8 Mastoid process.
of the Trunk.
9 7 Cervical Vertebrae.
10 First Dorsal Vertebra.
11 Twelfth do do.
12 First Lumbar do.
13 Os Sacrum.
14 Os Coccyx.
15 Os Ilium.
16 Crest of the Ilium.
17 Os pubis.
18 Os Ischium.
19 Sternum.
20 First rib.
21 Seventh & last true rib.
22 Two false ribs.
23 Collar bone.

A drawing by **Hamo Thornycroft** made to gain a studentship at the Royal Academy Antique School, 1869. 711 × 488 mm

The life class was a central part of artistic training, and was accompanied by lessons in human anatomy. It retained its importance as long as the primary aim of sculpture was to represent the range of human emotions by means of the human figure, in movement or at rest. Once a student had proved that he or she had mastered the figure, they were considered to be ready to make their own way in the wider professional world, where they would be judged by the effective marriage of the emotion to the figure.

The same pose, a classic one taken from Ancient Greek statuary, is shown in the pencil sketch of the Discobolus, or discus thrower, by W. F. Woodington. This is one of many sketches in one sketchbook, and they vary from romantic renderings of historical stories, to Bible scenes, to nude studies of the figure. In all they reveal the studies of a conscientious student, looking not only to master his means of expression, but also his appropriate treatment of well-known subjects.

Drawing of Myron's Discobolus figure in pencil by **W. F. Woodington** from sketchbook, *c.*1832. 353 × 256 mm

Sketches for sculpture from loose-leaved sketchbook
by **Austin Wright**, early 1970s. 445 × 550 mm

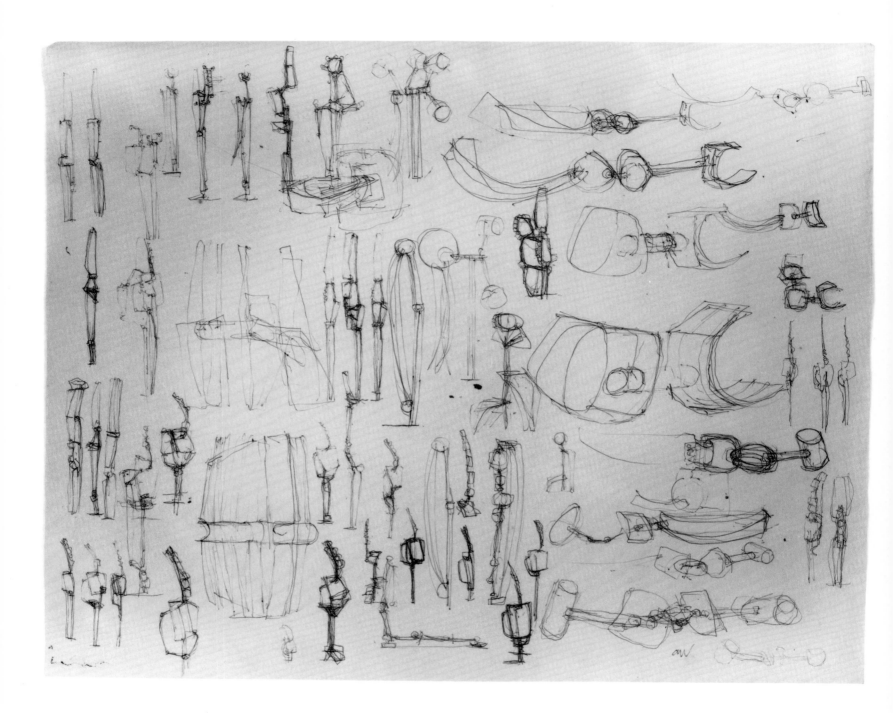

Most sculptors make drawings, and most sculptors keep sketchbooks. Sketchbooks are often valued by their owners above much of their larger, and more finished works, and it is one of the delights of the archive to be able to take a look at this private world. The page here is taken from one of the many sketchbooks compiled by Austin Wright. Wright's sketches are unusually close to his sculptures, and it is rewarding to be able to see an idea taking shape as it travels across the page. The drawings occupy the middle ground between the inspiration Wright took from landscape – bones, hills, rocks, trees – and his linear aluminium sculptures.

Business card and letter from **Auguste Rodin**
to **Jacob Epstein** from the Epstein archive, 1904.
53 × 87 mm & 167 × 123 mm

Young sculptors need friends, and the better placed on the professional
ladder, the more helpful those friends can prove to be. By the time that the
young Jacob Epstein met Rodin, Rodin was at the height of his international
fame, with a huge workshop and a famous clientele. Epstein must have
treasured his card.

Young sculptors graduate from art school having passed their final examinations. These exam papers show how different the assessment was only one generation ago. They were collected by the sculptor Eric Peskett, who taught at Bromley for nearly 40 years, a witness to the radical reshaping of art school education in post-war Britain. These students are asked to demonstrate their ability to provide sculpture with a social and architectural purpose, and within a strict time-limit.

Opposite

In the 19th and earlier 20th centuries the Royal Academy was accepted as an effective and worthwhile standard with little question. After leaving art school, it was the next step on the sculptor's ladder. Membership impressed not only your clients, but also your colleagues. It was a club to which one was honoured to be elected, and its annual exhibitions provided an important showcase and selling opportunity. This certificate records the award of its associate membership to the sculptor Henry Hugh Armstead.

Rules Governing the Award of the Ministry's Diplomas and Certificates in Art (HMSO London 1955). Three instruction sheets for *The examination for the national diploma in design* (Ministry of Education 1950, 1961 & 1964) from **Eric Peskett**'s archive. 213 × 136 mm & 245 × 154 mm (2x)

Opposite

Deed of inauguration, making **Henry Hugh Armstead** an associate member of the Royal Academy, 1875. 663 × 504 mm

Jacob Epstein at work on
'Behold the Man', *c*. 1935.
Jacob Epstein's studio with various
busts on a ladder and 'Venus', *c*. 1957.
177 × 250 mm & 295 × 188 mm

Armed with educational and professional qualifications, the sculptor has, most importantly, to establish his or her own professional practice. This would normally mean finding premises for a studio, and developing a reputation for a certain line of work; be it portraiture, decorative or architectural work. In the early years, most sculptors would work for another in order to pay their own rent. They too might employ their own juniors to help them out. As more jobs were taken on, so the studio workforce would increase, and if the jobs were complex, it would often divide, so that one assistant would work on carving, another on casting, and another on patinating. Though some work could be farmed out, it was also necessary to divide the studio into clean and dirty areas for different types of wet and dry work.

Galizia Foundry, casting ledger covering 1955–63 with photographs of work by Kenneth Armitage and Henry Moore, *c.* 1950s. 322 × 133 mm, 209 × 62 mm, 88 × 114 mm, & 100 × 77 mm

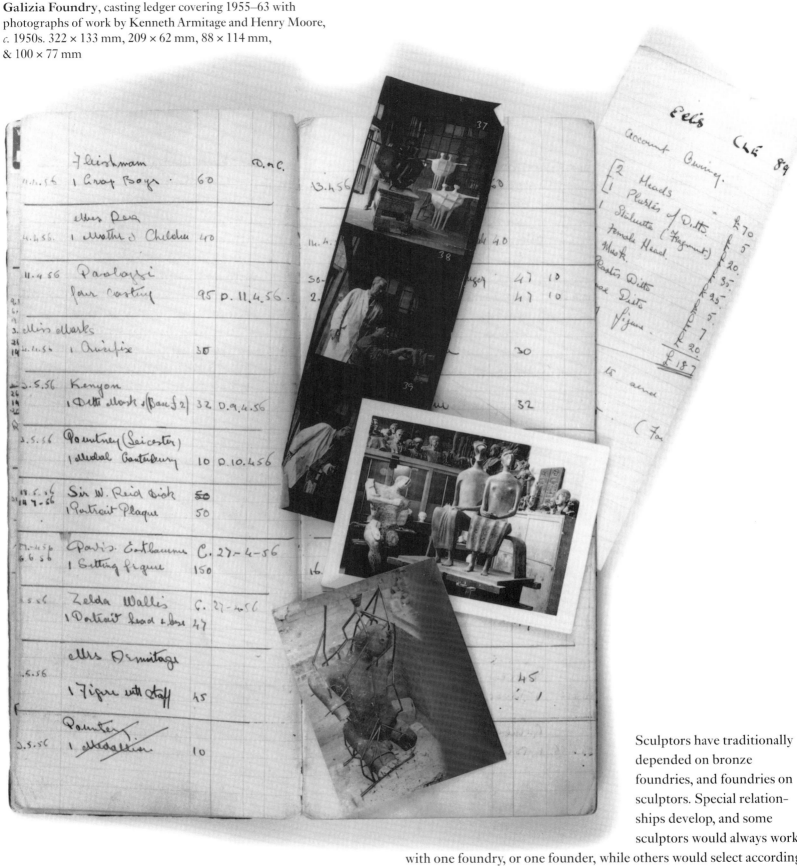

Sculptors have traditionally depended on bronze foundries, and foundries on sculptors. Special relationships develop, and some sculptors would always work with one foundry, or one founder, while others would select according to the type of work. As sculpture, and other trades, have diversified, foundries have closed down, and there are fewer today than earlier this century. The archive has the casting ledgers and account books, as well as some documentary photographs, from the Galizia Foundry in Battersea, London. They include famous names – Moore, Paolozzi, Armitage – along with the less famous – Nimptsch or Fleischmann – and many who are now quite forgotten.

Letter from
The Morris Singer
Company to
Laurence Bradshaw,
1953. 253 × 204 mm

THE MORRIS SINGER COMPANY
LIMITED
Incorporating William Morris & Company and J. W. Singer & Sons Ltd. of Frome

COLOSSAL STATUES AND
STATUETTES TABLETS AND
ARCHITECTURAL BRONZE WORK
BY SAND & CIRE PERDU PROCESS

DORSET ROAD, SOUTH LAMBETH. S.W.8
NEAR KENNINGTON OVAL TUBE STATION
CODES: LOMBARD AND BENTLEY'S SECOND
TELEPHONE   TELEGRAMS
RELIANCE 4129   MORISINGER WALT. LONDON

RFH/ALP/BMS. F.M. 1699   4th. November, 1953.

Captain George Pitt-Rivers

Laurence Bradshaw, Esq.,
22, Warwick Road,
London. S. W. 5.

Dear Sir,

          Further to our Mr. Parrott's call at your studio this
afternoon, we have pleasure in submitting the following estimate:-

Estimated cost of casting in bronze from plaster models
seen in your studio one Head 14" high x 9" across, one
Hand with sketch model 1' 0" long, and one Hand 6" long,
each casting to have an extension to act as a mount for
fixing to wood Bust, one button with chain and one without,
each with attachment for fixing. The work finished in
first class manner, toned golden colour, not waxed. Our
price includes for collecting plaster models from your
studio, and delivering bronze work, together with the
return of the plaster model, carriage paid.

                              £95. 0. 0d.

Delivery Seven weeks from receipt of models.

          This tender is based on today's costs and is subject to
adjustment in respect of any significant rise or fall in the cost
of Labour and/or Materials between the date of this tender and
completion of the contract.

          We hope to have the pleasure of carrying out this work on
your behalf.

                    Yours faithfully,
          THE MORRIS SINGER COMPANY LIMITED.
                    R. F. Howard. Director.

John Webb Singer set up a foundry in Frome, Somerset in the mid-nineteenth century. In the 1920s
it encountered competition in the shape of the newly established Morris Art Bronze Foundry, set up
through the William Morris Company. By 1927 The Morris Foundry had absorbed Singer's and the
new company took the name of Morris Singer and was based at the Morris premises in South
London. 45 years later they were obliged to leave their Lambeth premises and relocate in
Hampshire. The Morris Singer Company became the most famous foundry in Britain, and favoured
for some of the most ambitious commissions, for example by Barbara Hepworth.

Work in progress at
the **Galizia Foundry**,
n.d. 200 × 253 mm

These photographs from the
Galizia archives show part of
the process of pouring the
molten bronze into the
mould, and the runners
which allow the metal
through the outer casing
into the central hollow.
Some sculptors liked to keep
a close eye on the casting
process; others left it to the
foundry. Established
working relationships
allowed the founders to
know from experience what
their clients would want in
terms of chasing and
patinating the finished piece.

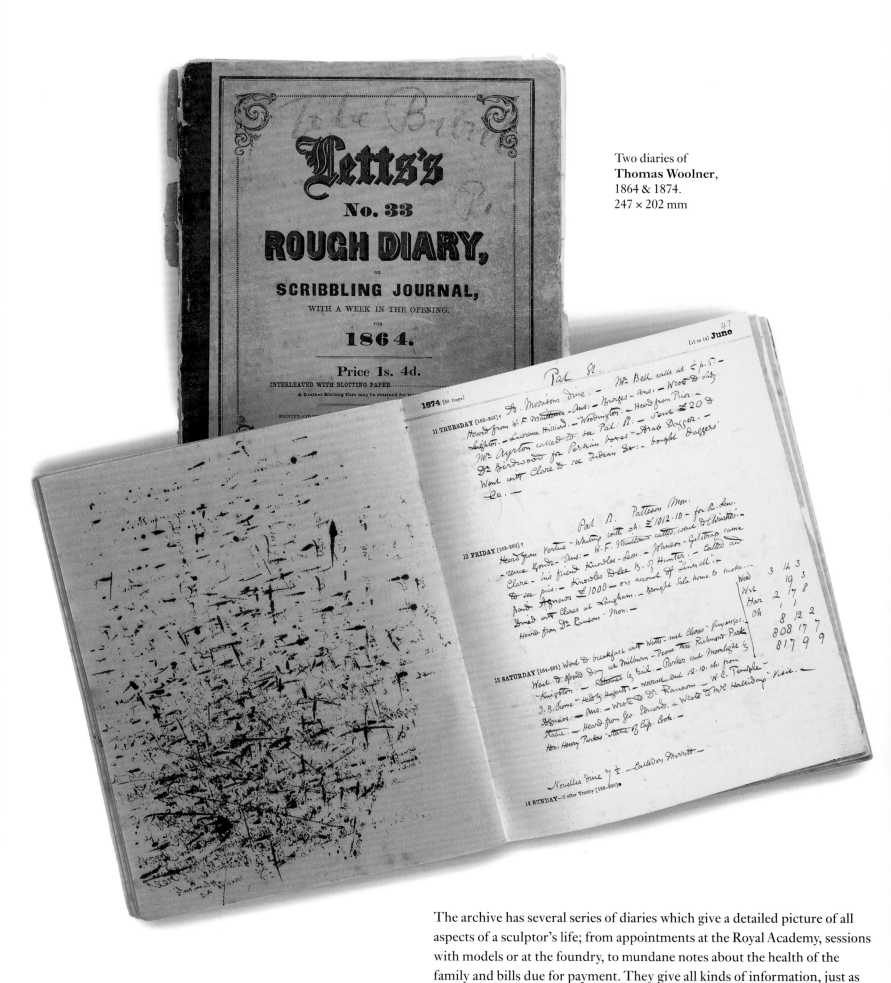

Two diaries of
Thomas Woolner,
1864 & 1874.
247 × 202 mm

The archive has several series of diaries which give a detailed picture of all aspects of a sculptor's life; from appointments at the Royal Academy, sessions with models or at the foundry, to mundane notes about the health of the family and bills due for payment. They give all kinds of information, just as much socio-historical as art-historical. These Letts scribbling diaries belonged to the Pre-Raphaelite sculptor Thomas Woolner.

Two letters from **Alfred Gilbert** to Douglas Illingworth,
1913 & 12. 274 × 210 mm & 220 × 177 mm

Casting was, and is, an expensive
business, only to be undertaken
when the concept and execution of a
piece was definitively realised.
Sculptors have often found
themselves unable ever to execute an
idea which was originally designed
to be cast, either through lack of
money, or through sheer perfec-
tionism. Alfred Gilbert, who writes
here from Belgium, where he had
taken refuge as a bankrupt, found
himself almost unable to commit
himself to sending his work to the
foundry, though as he tells his
British patron, Douglas Illingworth,
he is now on the point of doing so.

The scale of public statuary, particularly in its Victorian heyday, demanded specialist conditions of the artist's studio, and of the foundry. Despite the many assistants involved in the monumental process, the photographs in the archive tend to show the sculptor alone beside their work.

Hamo Thornycroft with the equestrian part of the monument to Cecil Rhodes for Kimberley – South Africa, *c.* 1907. 350 × 270 mm

Hamo Thornycroft's notebooks
1875 & 1873–83, diaries 1914, 1915,
1916 & 1916–19 and accounts 1916.
Smallest 100 × 703 mm, largest
180 × 120 mm

The Thornycroft archive is the largest single holding in the archive as a whole. Partly because of this, it is more wide-ranging, and goes into greater detail than the other papers. Though the holding represents a whole family of sculptors, it covers the life of Hamo Thornycroft in particular detail. Here are some of the many tiny pocket-books which he kept, and which are now preserved in Leeds. Though many of them, true to life, are only occasionally filled in, these ones rather poignantly evoke the long interval in ordinary working life that was the Great War.

The criteria by which sculpture was judged, particularly by the Academy, used to be absolute in a way that would be unthinkable today. Figurative sculpture could be seen to be well-modelled or badly modelled, and its presentation within a certain format and genre could be assessed on the quality of its interpretation. This photograph neatly conjures up the days when juries were all male, when sculpture was figurative, and when there were standards and principles held in common.

Photograph of
the Royal Academy
Selection Committee,
1933 from the
Ledward archive.
197 × 247 mm

Opposite

These *Notes on the Royal Academy Exhibition* remind us of how modest catalogues used to be, and also of the way in which sculpture used to be reproduced. Paintings have always been given more space than sculptures on the printed page. When illustrations were engraved paintings were reproduced more fully than sculptures; with the introduction of photography they were more successfully reproduced than sculpture, and, after the invention of colour photography, more often selected as deserving of colour than sculpture. The sculptures here are denoted by a kind of short-hand line, which may have encouraged the sculptors to think of profile and silhouette instead of interior modelling. However, it is also possible to make another argument, whereby sculpture has benefited from having escaped being successfully conquered by photography, and where the human interpretation, part and parcel of its representation on the page, adds life to the image itself.

Notes on the Royal Academy Exhibition, 1868,
pp. 28 & 29. *Academy Notes*, 1880, pp. 80 & xvii.
215 × 140 mm

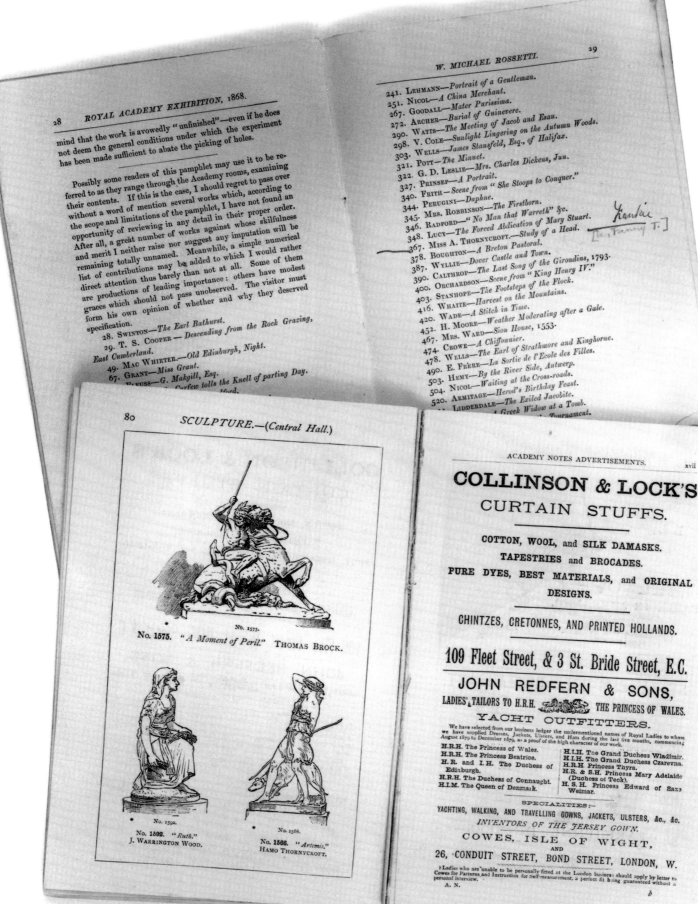

Maquette by **Arthur Fleischmann** for the 'Mermaid' (Lockheed Fountain) for the Festival of Britain, 1950. *Festival Pleasure Gardens* (London 1951), photograph and newspaper cutting of Arthur Fleischmann with the 20-year old model Joyce Taylor and the 'Mermaid', 1951. Page of magazine *The Motor* showing the 'Mermaid', 1951. 133 × 232 × 70 mm, 253 × 188 mm, 254 × 202 mm, 205 × 190 mm & 304 × 215 mm

This page sets up a whole narrative, culled from the souvenirs kept by the sculptor and his widow of a prestigious commission for the 1951 Festival of Britain. Press photographs, staged in the sculptor's studio, later appeared in a wide variety of newspapers, and the finished artwork itself also entered into the press in the form of advertising material. The Festival, a celebration of the country's return to peace, offered a wide variety of commissions to sculptors, most of which were removed when the temporary pavilions were demolished, and transferred to new homes round the country.

Portrait commissions were the stuff of many artists' lives, the backbone on which they depended to make a living. Like statues, though to a lesser extent, portraits had their own hierarchy, which one can see a successful portraitist like Epstein ascending as he models the Italian film star Gina Lollobrigida, or is asked to take on a commission for a royal portrait. Artists' relationships with particular models is of clear importance, artistically and emotionally. Photographs showing the posed female in the sculptor's studio play on the contrast between the ideal and the workaday.

University College of North Staffordshire

KEELE · STAFFORDSHIRE

Principal: *Sir George Barnes*, M.A., D.C.L.

Telephone: *Keele Park 371*

12th September, 1957.

Private & Confidential

Dear Sir Jacob,

Last year Princess Margaret became President of this new University College and installed me as Principal. The College wishes, early in Her Royal Highness's term of office, to commission a portrait of her. Would you be prepared to accept such a commission from the College, if Her Royal Highness's permission were to be obtained, and if so, what would be your fee for a bronze?

I spoke to Princess Margaret about this matter on her last visit, and obtained her approval to make this enquiry.

May I add how very much I hope that you would be willing to undertake this work. The College is already the fortunate possessor of a bronze head of yours "Isobel Elsom", which was presented to us by Dr. Barnett Stross three years ago.

Yours sincerely,

George Barnes

Sir Jacob Epstein, K.B.E., LL.D., D.C.L.,
18 Hyde Park Gate,
London, S.W.7.

Letter to **Jacob Epstein** from the principal of the University of North Staffordshire about the possible commission of a bust of the newly appointed president – Princess Margaret, 1957.
Photograph of Epstein sculpting
Gina Lollobrigida, 1952. 252 × 201 mm
& 158 × 149 mm

Artists need to sell works. Sculpture can take a very long time to make, and is an expensive business. One way of recouping costs was to exploit the possibilities of bronze, and to make an edition for sale. While typical edition sizes are around ten to a dozen, some pieces – and perhaps particularly commemorative busts or miniature statues, and decorative statuettes – had such good sales potential that they were made in very large editions. Such wholesale exploitation was made possible by the industrializing of the art bronze industry, and later in the century, many sculptors reacted against this, and promoted the uniqueness of the hand-finished item.

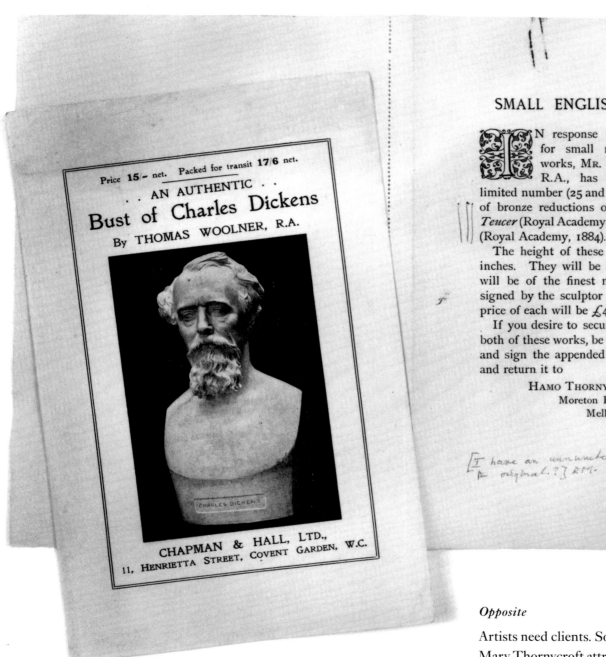

SMALL ENGLISH BRONZES.

IN response to repeated inquiries for small reproductions of his works, MR. HAMO THORNYCROFT, R.A., has decided to issue a limited number (25 and no more in each case) of bronze reductions of two of his statues, *Teucer* (Royal Academy, 1882) and *The Mower* (Royal Academy, 1884).

The height of these statuettes will be 22 inches. They will be cast in England, and will be of the finest metal. Each will be signed by the sculptor and numbered. The price of each will be £40.

If you desire to secure a copy of either or both of these works, be kind enough to fill up and sign the appended form of subscription, and return it to

HAMO THORNYCROFT, R.A.,
Moreton House,
Melbury Road, Kensington,
London, W.

Leaflet offering copies of 'Teucer' and 'The Mower' by **Hamo Thornycroft** for sale, *c.* 1889. 210 × 150 mm.
Posthumous leaflet offering copies for sale of the 'Charles Dickens' bust by **Thomas Woolner**, *c.* 1890s. The bust was originally produced in 1872. 216 × 139 mm

Opposite

Artists need clients. Some are richer than others. Mary Thornycroft attracted praise for her work at an early stage in her career, and was fortunate to enjoy the patronage of the Royal Family. Such patronage existed first and foremost within the field of portraiture, as the Privy Purse was well able to pay for the busts of members of the extensive family network. Queen Victoria was noted for her interest in sculpture, and certain sculptors basked in the security of her favours. Moreover, a number of her own family circle trained and practised as semi-professional sculptors.

Photograph of **Mary Thornycroft** in front of the statue of Princess Helena, 1855. Receipt from Mary Thornycroft to Her Majesty's Privy Purse for £100 for a marble bust of HRH Princess Alice and a bronze head of a horse, 1862. 336 × 302 mm & 81 × 167 mm

Photographs of works by **Gilbert Ledward** and various sculptors associated with the company 'Sculptured Memorials and Headstones' founded by Ledward in 1934. The company's headquarters moved during the Second World War to Gill's home in Buckinghamshire. The photographs show: headstones 200 × 140 mm, 156 × 118 mm & 200 × 78 mm. Letter by **Eric Gill** to **Joseph Cribb**, 1927. 247 × 174 mm

Aside from portraiture from the living model, another sure source of income for the sculptor was in commemorative and funerary works. The grander of these works might involve a commemorative bust, or even a statue, but more often simply required of the sculptor a tablet, an inscription, a passage of decorative carving, or simply a carved headstone. Eric Gill began his working life as a monumental mason, and though he extended his skill in stone into fully three-dimensional 'fine-art' carving, he always retained his interest in well-set lettering. In the 1930s sculptors suffered, along with everyone else, from the recession, and found ways to use their skills more commercially. These gravestones are examples from a whole range offered by the 'Sculptured Memorials and Headstones' company.

Henry Wood of Bristol showing one page from an album of designs for funerary monuments, *c.* late 18th to early 19th century. 425 × 550 mm

Though painted rather than photographed, this page from Wood's 'Monumental Masonry' offers a similar service. The page is one of many in the album, through which a bereaved family, or even a prospective client, could browse in order to gauge the range of styles available, and the scale of associated costs. The variations on offer range from a very simple tablet, to a large relief composition complete with mourning figures. Making a profit in sculpture was a difficult business, partly because clients never understood how expensive were the materials and the labour. Offering a 'sales catalogue' was a way of ensuring that the sculptor did not sell himself too cheap, and that the client was less likely to be disappointed. Some of the common components of the designs would be kept in stock in the workshop, so that bespoke work – to individual specifications – could be kept to a minimum.

View of Crystal Palace at Sydenham (*c.*1854) contained in the 1862
International Exhibition photograph album. 215 × 275 mm

Another – but more precarious – way of seeking fame and fortune was to chance the exhibition
halls. Though the 19th century saw many fewer individual exhibitions than now, and though the
commercial gallery system had hardly seen the light of day, there was a range of exhibiting
societies, which had their annual shows, crowned by the Royal Academy, the various Paris
Salons, and the wave of International Exhibitions which incorporated sections devoted to
sculpture. However, as these photographs show, it was hard to shine in a hall filled with
sculpture – mostly in white plaster – all of it waiting to strike someone's eye before it could come
to life in a more permanent form; in bronze or marble. Such uniformity pushed some sculptors
to develop strategies to make their pieces stand out from the crowd, but despite the medals and
accolades that came with such occasions, the atmosphere of the World's Fair was fundamentally
hostile to individual works.

The International Exhibitions were accompanied by a range of publications, from luxury souvenir catalogues to modest pamphlets, and their subjects were divided in different ways, either by country, because national competition was an inherent part of the exercise, or by material, or by art form. These pages, brought back from Paris, show how sculptures – like other items – were reduced to long lists, with only a few works being singled out for special treatment by the illustrator.

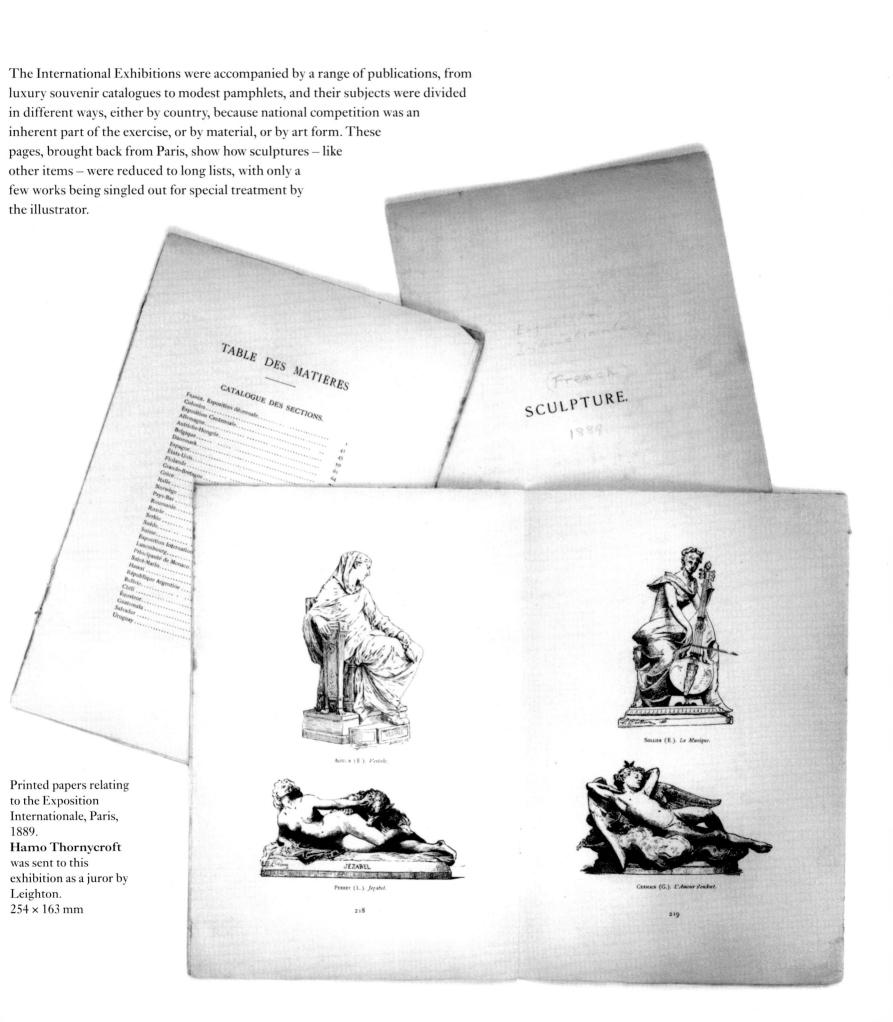

Printed papers relating to the Exposition Internationale, Paris, 1889.
Hamo Thornycroft was sent to this exhibition as a juror by Leighton.
254 × 163 mm

Architectural decoration had long been a stock in trade
for the sculptor, and it is only since the Second World War that this aspect has died away
from both the sculptor's training, and the range of career options. Sculptors' work on the facades of our cities –
banks, civic buildings, art galleries – is all around us. Sculptors trained to work with and for architects were thus well able to rise
to the occasion when national pride demanded splendid – if temporary – show-piece decorations. The Coronation of 1937 was just
such a cause, and the occasion is recorded here by Selfridges department store, in a souvenir leaflet documenting an ambitious frieze
along the store's facade on London's Oxford Street. Although the occasion was special, and though the decorations were only temporary,
they are by some of the most well-respected academic sculptors of the time, and entirely in keeping with the style of more permanent work.

A portfolio of Selfridge's decorations for the coronation of HM King George VI and HM Queen Elizabeth, 1937. Various artists worked on the project including **Hermon Cawthra**. The central group was developed by J. A. Stevenson from a sketch model by William Reid Dick. 374 × 999 mm & 379 × 254 mm. This document is part of the Cawthra archive

Exhibiting work could, on occasion, bring fame, or notoriety, and Epstein experienced both. With the growth of the private gallery system, and with it the opportunity to present a single artist's work, individual sculptors could be more readily positioned by the Press. Though the previous centuries had perhaps primarily judged their best sculptors by offering them challenging commissions for monumental work, the 20th century has tended to judge them by groups of sculptures shown within the context of a solo exhibition. In Britain the reputations of Epstein, and then of Moore, were very much created by means of this system. Both were lampooned for their early shows, but later became national celebrities. Epstein's works received different kinds of attention according to whether they were modelled or carved; here he is seen as the object of 'media' attention in a private London gallery, while in Blackpool the crowds gather to assess for themselves the scandalous nature of his monumental carving 'Adam'.

Photograph of the crowds queuing to see 'Adam' in Blackpool, 1939. Photograph of **Jacob Epstein** with bust of 'Isobel' in a Leicester Galleries show, *c.* 1930s. 375 × 264 mm & 188 × 246 mm

Preparing work for exhibitions has increasingly, since the early 20th century, taken up the sculptor's time. Whereas exhibitions used to involve a jury, and only one or two pieces from each artist, it is now an opportunity to present a whole body of work, as a kind of definitive personal statement. The very fact that sculptures can take a very long time to make can be worrying to sculptors, afraid of not having enough ready to make a good showing. If an artist is represented in several exhibitions at once, the pool of 'available' work dries up, and sculptors may be forced to show earlier work, if they don't borrow back from clients and collections. Whether to concentrate on one exhibition, or to show in several, can be a hard policy decision, and may depend as much on questions of obligation, or local connections, as on prestige. For an artist like Barbara Hepworth, hundreds of miles away from an exhibiting centre, the worries were more intense.

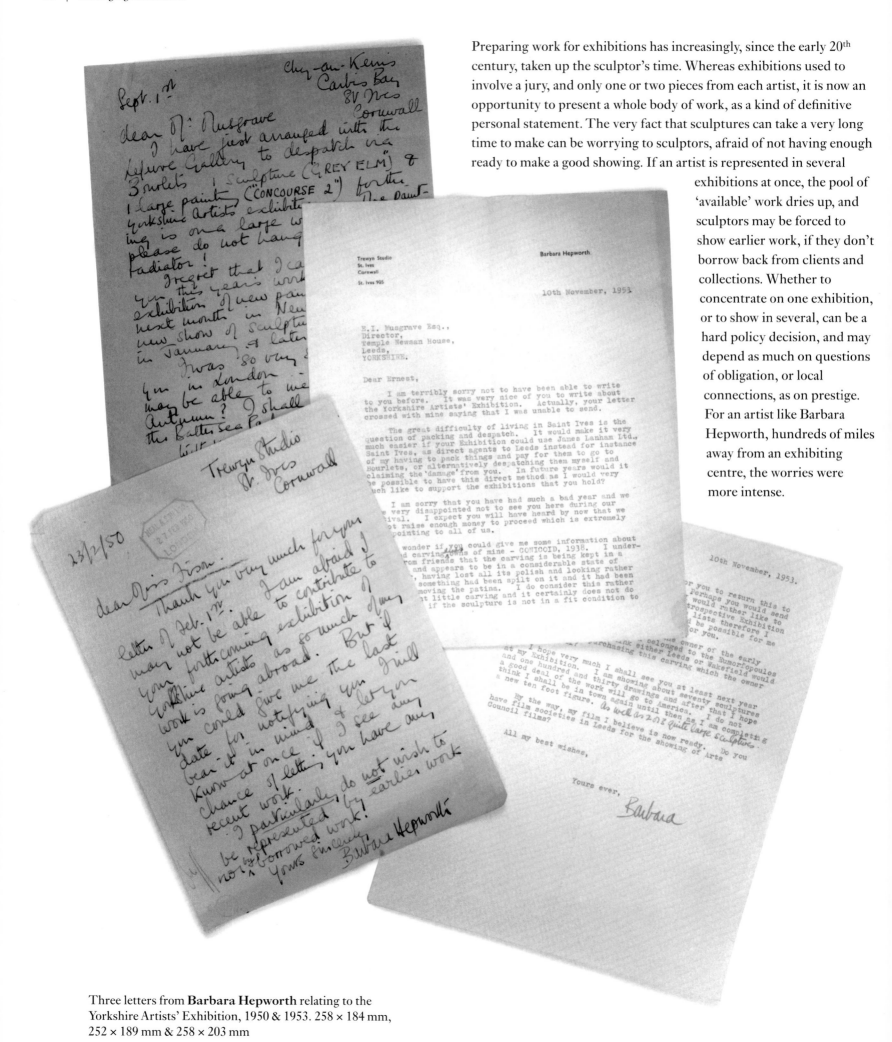

Three letters from **Barbara Hepworth** relating to the Yorkshire Artists' Exhibition, 1950 & 1953. 258 × 184 mm, 252 × 189 mm & 258 × 203 mm

Making exhibitions, particularly for sculptors, has increasingly become involved with the physical qualities of the exhibition space itself. Even if works are not 'site-specific', made for and about one particular site, sculptors almost invariably think very carefully about the nature of the space where they are going to show. Apart from obvious considerations, like the height of the ceiling, or the width of the door, sculptors look to the quality of the light, the flooring, and the feel in general, as well as to more detailed features, such as a skirting board. Many sculptors have thus adapted their working practice to making work specifically for a space, and even to making their work in that space. David Nash has developed a particular exhibition-making approach, whereby he makes his work 'on location', in the weeks leading up to a show, and lives and works in close contact with the exhibition space, so that he can 'get it right'. These sketches show him envisaging his sculptures in the space, and also the lay-out of his catalogue.

Letter to **David Nash** from the curator of the Center of Contemporary Art, Ujazdowski Castle, dummy catalogue and sketchbook relating to David Nash's Polish project, 1990–1991. 300 × 210 mm, 107 × 149 mm & 406 × 304 mm

Raising monuments to the respected dead became a way of life in Victorian Britain, and though the practice declined in the 20th century, two world wars ensured the continuance of at least that branch of commemorative practice. Monuments were usually raised by subscription, with an executive committee who organised the fund-raising and oversaw the selection of the sculptor. The letters here are typical of the life of the committee. Such monuments were so common in late 19th century Europe and America that sculptors could set up the complex and costly workshops needed for their execution, secure in the knowledge that they would receive sufficient commissions to keep them, and their assistants, in business for the whole of their careers. In the succeeding decades this practice has depended more on the unique character of the person to be commemorated, on a particularly powerful committee, or on the fame of the artist .

Internal correspondence between members of the W. H. Hudson Memorial Executive Committee about the **Epstein** commission for the monument in Hyde Park, 1923. 259 × 208 mm

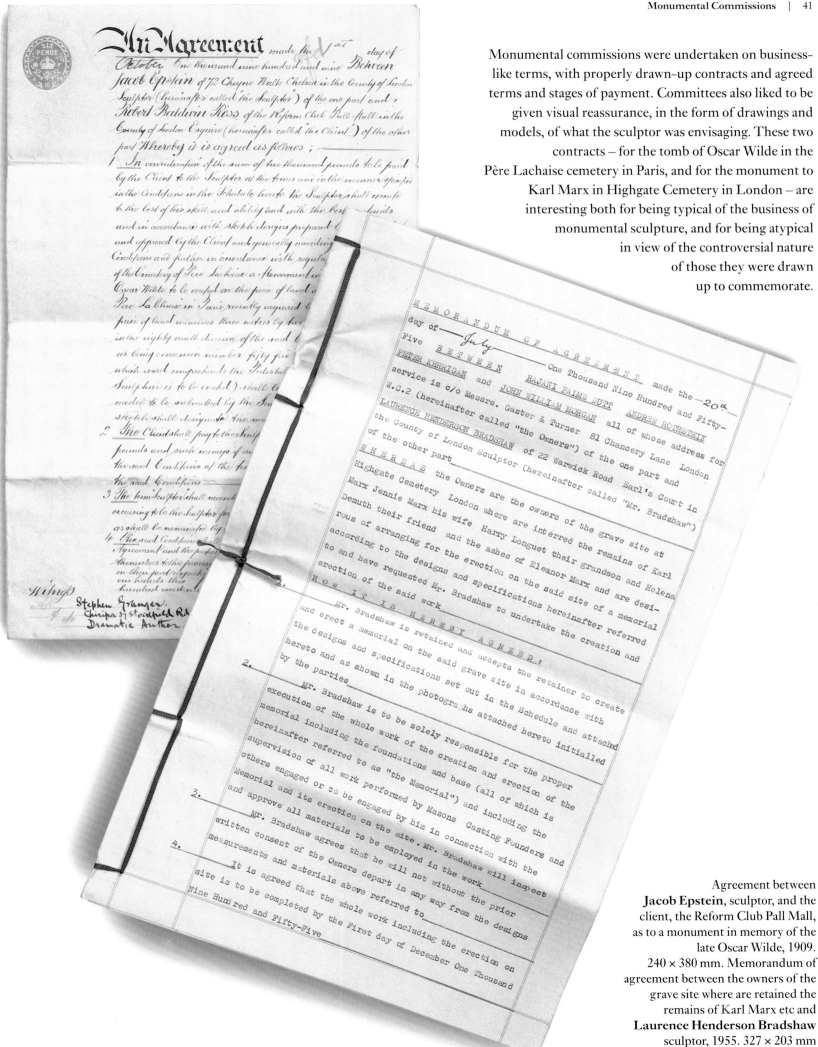

Monumental commissions were undertaken on business-like terms, with properly drawn-up contracts and agreed terms and stages of payment. Committees also liked to be given visual reassurance, in the form of drawings and models, of what the sculptor was envisaging. These two contracts – for the tomb of Oscar Wilde in the Père Lachaise cemetery in Paris, and for the monument to Karl Marx in Highgate Cemetery in London – are interesting both for being typical of the business of monumental sculpture, and for being atypical in view of the controversial nature of those they were drawn up to commemorate.

Agreement between **Jacob Epstein**, sculptor, and the client, the Reform Club Pall Mall, as to a monument in memory of the late Oscar Wilde, 1909. 240 × 380 mm. Memorandum of agreement between the owners of the grave site where are retained the remains of Karl Marx etc and **Laurence Henderson Bradshaw** sculptor, 1955. 327 × 203 mm

The belief that a given cause, an individual or a group, was worthy of being remembered in permanent form, by means of a monument, was not in itself enough. Once the committee was set up, the sculptor selected, and the contract drawn up, the fund-raising began in earnest. Committees used all the familiar ways of raising money; grants, personal subscriptions, small-scale editions of the model, lotteries, galas and dinners. Some causes – very famous characters, tragic loss of life – attracted the requisite sums with little difficulty. Other campaigns might drag on for years, either causing the artist to reduce the scope and ambition of the project, or necessitating the selection of another artist, and might even end in failure, resulting in the wholesale abandon of the project.

THE MARX MONUMENT COMMITTEE announces final plans for the erection of a monument to Karl Marx over his new grave at Highgate Cemetery. The monument will be in the form of a bust: illustrations of the approved model are on the front and back cover of this folder.

The new site is more appropriate in its environment for the erection of the proposed monument, and more convenient as a place of pilgrimage for the hundreds of visitors from all lands who yearly visit the cemetery for this purpose.

It is more than seventy years since Jenny von Westphalen, the beloved wife of Karl Marx, was buried in Highgate Cemetery, and a simple tablet bearing her name was placed over the grave. On this tablet were subsequently inscribed the names of Marx himself, his infant grandson Harry Longuet and the family's devoted servant and friend Helena Demuth. This tablet, familiar to visitors since 1883, is being incorporated in the plinth, as will be seen from the photographs; and it will also bear the name of Marx's gifted daughter Eleanor, whose ashes have been buried beside her parents.

The cost of executing the monument in materials at once handsome and durable—Westmorland slate and bronze—is in itself considerable: but the acquisition of a new site has involved additional expenditure of more than £2,500. Our earlier appeal (1950) brought just enough to cover the initial cost. A further sum of £10,000 is required to cover all expenses.

The Marx Monument Committee appeals with confidence to those organisations and individuals who revere the name of Karl Marx, teacher of the working class and founder of scientific Socialism, to contribute generously to the Fund. Sums large and small should be sent with the form below to the Hon. Treasurer, Marx Monument Fund.

On behalf of the Marx Monument Committee:

John W. Morgan. Hon. Secretary.

A. Horner Hon. Treasurer.

To Arthur L. Horner, Hon. Treasurer, Marx Monument Fund, Marx House, 37a Clerkenwell Green, London, E.C.1.

I enclose cheque, postal order* for £   being a contribution to the Marx Monument Fund on behalf of my organisation, myself.*   *Please cross out which does not apply.*

Please make cheques payable to The Marx Monument Fund and crossed.

Organisation or Contributor ....

Secretary's Name ....

Address ....

....

Date ....   *Signature* ....

Appeal leaflet for contributions to the Marx Monument Fund, *c.* 1955. 356 × 203 mm

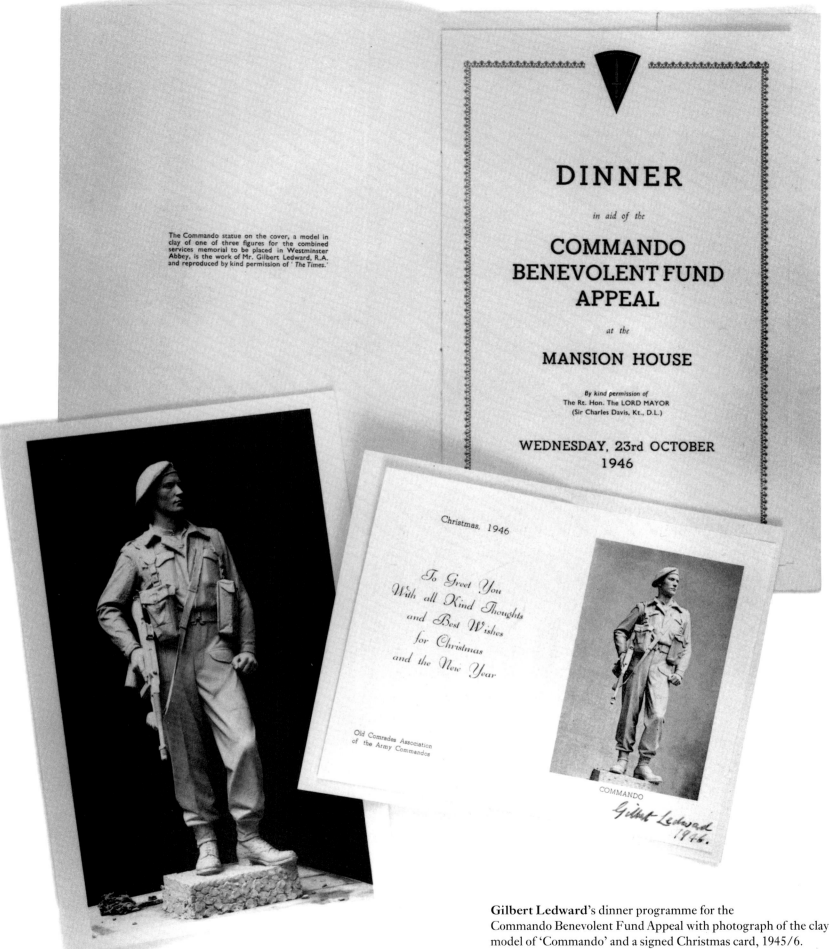

The Commando statue on the cover, a model in clay of one of three figures for the combined services memorial to be placed in Westminster Abbey, is the work of Mr. Gilbert Ledward, R.A. and reproduced by kind permission of 'The Times.'

DINNER

in aid of the

COMMANDO BENEVOLENT FUND APPEAL

at the

MANSION HOUSE

By kind permission of
The Rt. Hon. The LORD MAYOR
(Sir Charles Davis, Kt., D.L.)

WEDNESDAY, 23rd OCTOBER 1946

Christmas, 1946

To Greet You
With all Kind Thoughts
and Best Wishes
for Christmas
and the New Year

Old Comrades Association
of the Army Commandos

COMMANDO

Gilbert Ledward 1946.

Gilbert Ledward's dinner programme for the Commando Benevolent Fund Appeal with photograph of the clay model of 'Commando' and a signed Christmas card, 1945/6. 238 × 151 mm, 213 × 133 mm & 140 × 86 mm. The War Memorial to the Submarine Service, Commandos and Airborne Forces is located in the cloister of Westminster Abbey and was unveiled by Sir Winston Churchill in 1948

One page of sketches by **Peter Laszlo Peri** showing ideas for school sculptures, *c.* 1950s. Realised sculptures which can be related to the sketches are 'Children reading together' at Earl Shilton Grammar School, 'Reclining boy and girl' at Hinckley College and 'Girl reading a book' at Hatfield High School. Maquette called 'Boy and Girl examing a flask', *c.* 1950s. 278 × 386 mm & 180 × 460 × 160 mm

After the Second World War Britain saw a new wave of public sculpture, but public sculpture with a difference. It was no longer dedicated to the memory of a great lost hero or politician, and no longer sited in the most public squares of the city. This new sculpture, in keeping with the mood of left-wing reconstruction of a war-damaged society, portrayed the ordinary man, woman or child, and was placed in the courtyards of the housing estates in London and the New Towns, in schools and colleges. Some of those sculptors who had fled Central Europe just before the outbreak of war were particularly prominent within this movement. This sheet of sketches is one of many in which the Hungarian-born sculptor Peri essays different arrangements of a sculpture for a school. The maquette might have served as a private model, or as an example the sculptor would have taken to the commissioning committee to show them what he was proposing.

The monumental process was a long one, and required a good degree of trust and understanding between the sculptor and the commissioning committee. Projects could be abandoned if the committee thought the sculptor was trying to go beyond what they had originally agreed, or if the sculptor felt fundamentally undermined by the committee. However, the nature of making this kind of sculpture, with its different stages, from the small scale initial conception, through the scaling-up, preparation of moulds and casting, allowed an anxious committee a number of opportunities to check that they were going to get what they wanted.

Four photographs showing different phases in the development of 'The Seer' by **Gilbert Ledward**, *c.* 1957. The fourth photograph shows 'The Seer' in its location in the forecourt of Mercury House, Knightbridge. 210 × 165 mm, 205 × 166 mm, 153 × 205 mm, 213 × 163 mm

Although modernist sculptors were keen to free themselves from what they saw as a fatal partnership with architects, there were many sculptors who believed that this social exercise of the sculptor's skills, conditioned by function and fitness of purpose, was in fact sculpture's highest goal. Those sculptors who were genuinely interested in collaboration, in anonymity rather than individualist prowess – many of them members of the Art Workers Guild – were naturally happy to be involved in architectural schemes, while for others, it was simply the bread-and-butter of their working lives. Satisfactory outcomes, for both sides, normally depended in the end more on good working relationships than on idealistic beliefs that were notionally held in common.

Designs and blue print for bronze door for the Guildhall in Cambridge. by **Laurence Bradshaw**, *c.* 1935–8. 760 × 1270 mm, 358 × 261 mm & 384 × 276 mm

Two photographs showing **Gilbert Ledward** with one of his later works, Barclays Bank DCO, Old Broad St, London. It shows the half-size clay model and the half finished work, *c.* 1958–9. One photograph showing work in progress on the Adelphi building, London, *c.* 1937. 207 × 155 mm, 203 × 250 mm, 206 × 169 mm

The marriage between the architect and the sculptor is often forgotten nowadays, but photographs like these, showing the sculptor actually on the scaffolding, bring the alliance vividly to life. Some sculptors really did finish off their work on the building site, while others would send workmen up in their place, working from models. Some such photos would be staged for the press, or for posterity, because the bulk of the work would normally be done in the studio, and only a very few sculptors made a point of making their work absolutely integral with the building's facade.

Photograph of the unveiling of
Gilbert Ledward's Guards' Division
Memorial unveiled by HRH The Duke
of Connaught at the Horse Guards
Parade, London, 1926. 248 × 396 mm.
The unveiling of the South African War
Memorial to the 'Lancashire Fusiliers'
made by **George Frampton** and
unveiled by HM King George V in
1905. 251 × 302 mm

The unveiling ceremony is a
symbol, a ritual in the process of
monumental statuary. Though many
members of the public would
already have seen the statue as it was
being erected, it was made secret
again before its official inauguration.
Some sculptors did set great store
by secrecy, and insisted that their
work only be erected under cover of
darkness, or behind hoardings. The
unveiling officially transferred the
monument out of the hands of the
executive committee, and into the
hands of its public. It was thus a real
– if only vaguely understood –
transferral of ownership. The author
of the work – the sculptor – often failed to even get a mention in such
ceremonies, though the increasing individual fame of the practitioners
could secure a reference.

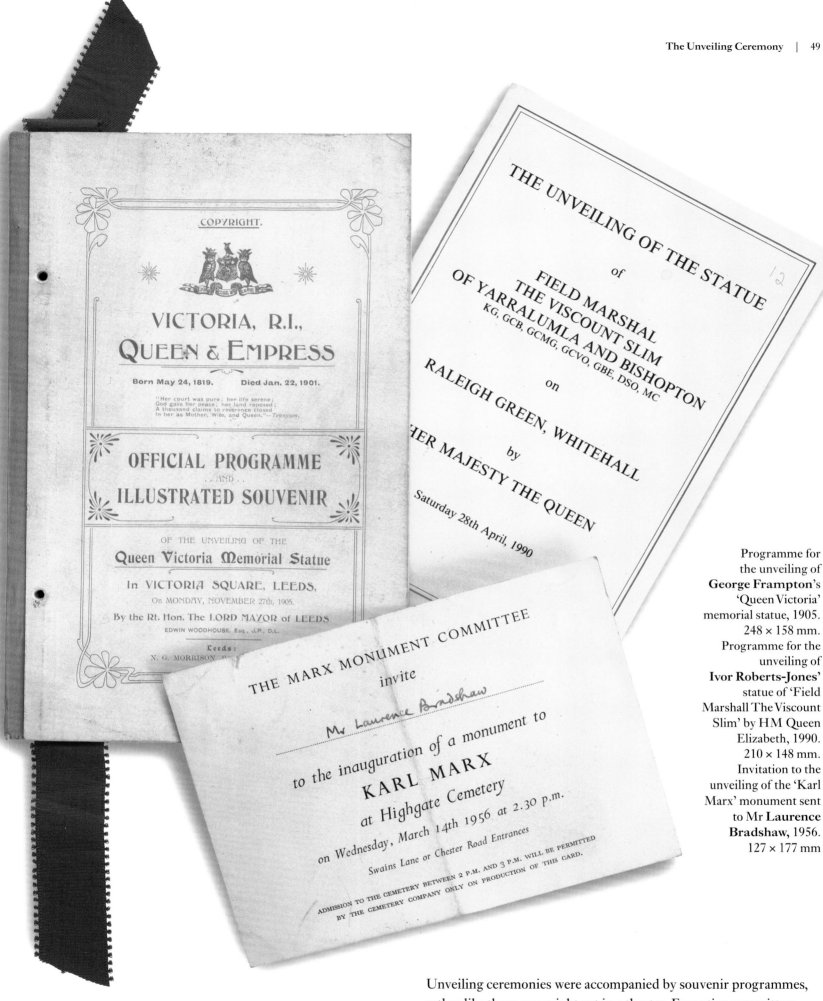

COPYRIGHT.

VICTORIA, R.I.,
QUEEN & EMPRESS

Born May 24, 1819.   Died Jan. 22, 1901.

"Her court was pure; her life serene;
God gave her peace; her land reposed;
A thousand claims to reverence closed
In her as Mother, Wife, and Queen."—*Tennyson*.

OFFICIAL PROGRAMME
..AND..
ILLUSTRATED SOUVENIR

OF THE UNVEILING OF THE

Queen Victoria Memorial Statue

In VICTORIA SQUARE, LEEDS,
On MONDAY, NOVEMBER 27th, 1905.

By the Rt. Hon. The LORD MAYOR of LEEDS
EDWIN WOODHOUSE, Esq., J.P., D.L.

Leeds:
N. G. MORRISON,

THE UNVEILING OF THE STATUE
of
FIELD MARSHAL
THE VISCOUNT SLIM
OF YARRALUMLA AND BISHOPTON
KG, GCB, GCMG, GCVO, GBE, DSO, MC

on

RALEIGH GREEN, WHITEHALL

by

HER MAJESTY THE QUEEN

Saturday 28th April, 1990

THE MARX MONUMENT COMMITTEE
invite

Mr Laurence Bradshaw

to the inauguration of a monument to
KARL MARX
at Highgate Cemetery

on Wednesday, March 14th 1956 at 2.30 p.m.

Swains Lane or Chester Road Entrances

ADMISSION TO THE CEMETERY BETWEEN 2 P.M. AND 3 P.M. WILL BE PERMITTED
BY THE CEMETERY COMPANY ONLY ON PRODUCTION OF THIS CARD.

Programme for the unveiling of **George Frampton**'s 'Queen Victoria' memorial statue, 1905. 248 × 158 mm. Programme for the unveiling of **Ivor Roberts-Jones'** statue of 'Field Marshall The Viscount Slim' by HM Queen Elizabeth, 1990. 210 × 148 mm. Invitation to the unveiling of the 'Karl Marx' monument sent to Mr **Laurence Bradshaw**, 1956. 127 × 177 mm

Unveiling ceremonies were accompanied by souvenir programmes, rather like those one might get in a theatre. Executive committees sought to secure the services of a celebrity to perform the unveiling, and often arranged music and decorations in addition to the speeches, as well as catering and even, on occasion, time-off and transport to enable the town's workforce to attend the ceremony.

Page of **Hamo Thornycroft**'s studio diary and sketches showing how the statue of Queen Victoria was meant to be erected in Durban, South Africa. The sketches were made on the day the statue was packed for shipping, 1899. 284 × 215 mm

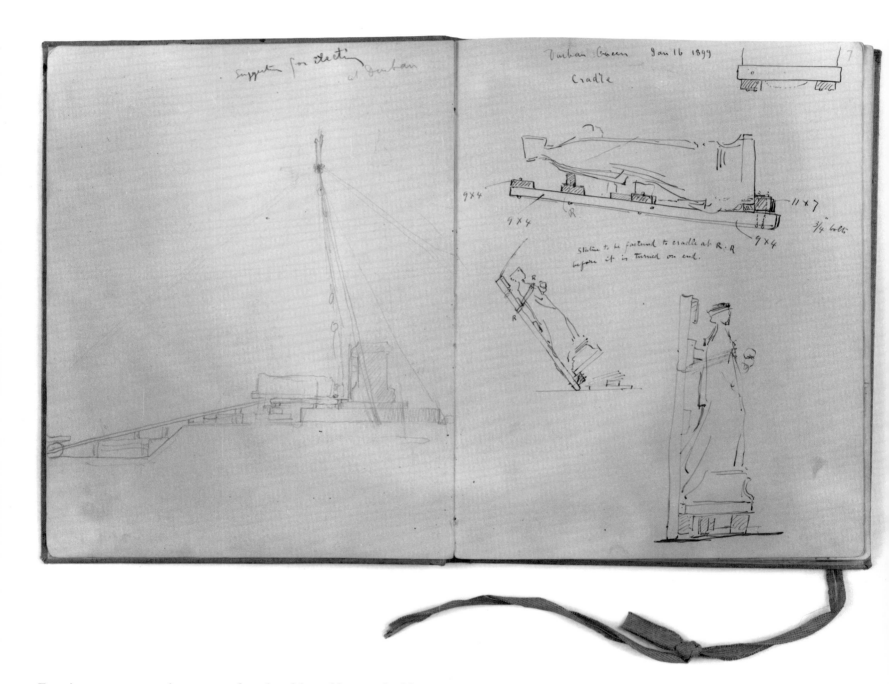

Erecting a monumental statue was fraught with problems and with potential risks. Even when sites had been carefully selected and surveyed, and appropriate foundations laid, things could go wrong at the last minute. The monumental sculptor needed to be something of a structural engineer to understand how the work would withstand pressure, and how best to lever it into position. Very often, and particularly in the context of the British Empire, the sculptor would not be present at the erection or the unveiling of the work, and thus could only supply notes and drawings so as to inform the local workforce about recommended approaches.

Photographs of 'King Alfred', a work by **Hamo Thornycroft**, about to be lifted onto its pedestal in Winchester. The attempt did not succeed the first time and slightly damaged the work, 1901. 104 × 138 mm & 200 × 151 mm

Documentary photographs of the erection and unveiling of monuments remind us of the pre-life of the statues which still people our streets. After their inaugurations they became 'public', but preceding this moment were months, and often years of a private life in the sculptor's studio. After a long gestation, during which the sculptor feels that he or she owns the work, while the committee feels the same, and has more right in law, the work is brought out into the cold light of day and has to go through yet another indignity, that of being hauled into position, before it can be discreetly veiled in flags or drapery.

Cards and invitations to
private views relating to
exhibitions by Hans Arp,
1950–1986. The cards are
from the **Paule Vézelay**
archive.
Smallest 125 × 105 mm
& largest 139 × 200 mm

Sculptors' works and careers live on in a number of ways. The supposedly permanent markers which are the works on our streets, and on the buildings which flank them, are all but invisible to most of those who walk by them. It is the exhibition, and its accompanying publications, which are now most effective at promoting a sculptor's oeuvre. Unused as we are to assessing the sculpture on our streets, and unused as the sculptors of the past were to the paraphernalia which now surrounds the exhibition, it is small wonder that so many sculptors' careers survive only in the archive. Modernist sculptors built their careers on the exhibition, and their catalogues are in our libraries, and they continue to feature in contemporary exhibition-making. The exhibition is a phenomenon in itself, with its press releases, private view cards, opening dinners, posters and postcards reminiscent of the equally complex formulas surrounding the monument. Artists set great store by the design and dissemination of the announcement cards for their exhibitions, and the work of Arp was so suitable to graphic reproduction that cards advertising exhibitions of his work retain a uniformity even after his death.

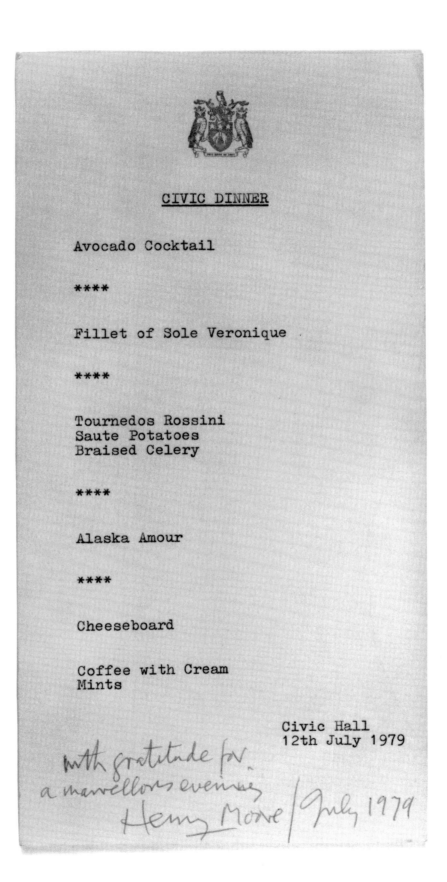

Menu for a dinner at Leeds Civic Hall with message from **Henry Moore**, 1979. 230 × 116 mm

Celebrated artists are offered dinners by town councils, municipalities, and city fathers in honour of their achievements. Such dinners often coincide with the opening of an exhibition, especially if the artist is a local one, whom the city council finally wishes to claim as its own.

Tributes to artists after their death come in various ways; in the form of memorial services, fellowships, lectures and retrospective exhibitions. Only the very famous are paid tributes such as a Memorial Concert at the Tate Gallery.

TATE GALLERY
Millbank, S.W.1

by kind permission of the Trustees

Friday, November 10, at 8 p.m.

Epstein *1961*
Memorial Concert

to be held during the Arts Council's

EPSTEIN MEMORIAL EXHIBITION
(November 3 — December 17)

MARIA DONSKA	**CHRISTOPHER BUNTING**
Pianoforte	Violoncello
ILSE WOLF	**RAYMOND LEPPARD**
Soprano	Pianoforte

A limited number of tickets available at £3.3.0

(To include Champagne Supper and a Private View of the Exhibition)

Obtainable from
IBBS AND TILLETT LTD., 124 Wigmore Street, W.1
Ticket Office: WELbeck 8418 Hours: 10-5, Saturdays 10-12

Postal applications for tickets should be accompanied by a stamped, addressed envelope

---

Leaflet advertising the Epstein Memorial concert at the Tate Gallery, 1961. **Jacob Epstein** died in 1959. 228 × 142 mm

---

Opposite

In the days before the illustrated exhibition catalogue, which is now run of the mill, the art press, and especially the dedicated monthly journals, were all the more important in disseminating information about the current work of artists, and movements within artistic circles. Here the *Art Journal*, central to artistic discussion of the time, dedicates a whole edition to celebrating the life and work of Alfred Gilbert. This was the initiative of one of the artist's closest friends, and thought it came dangerously close to the obituary, was intended to keep the artist (living in Belgium) in the public eye. The special interview which Gilbert conceded to give for the occasion now stands as one of the texts most revealing of the artist.

The Easter edition of the *Art Journal* concentrating on the life and work of **Alfred Gilbert**, then aged 49. 1903. 341 × 260 mm

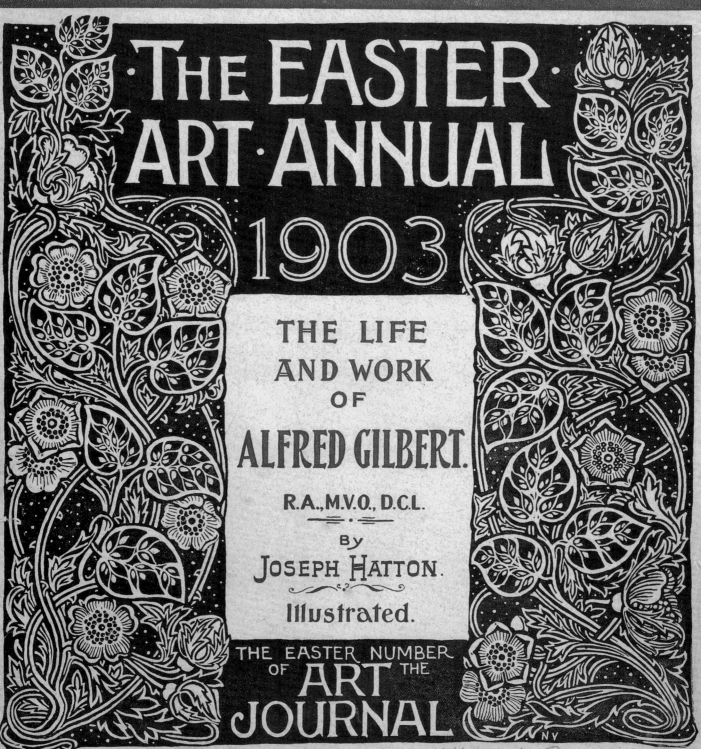

PRICE HALF-A-CROWN.

ALFRED GILBERT R.A.

· THE EASTER · ART · ANNUAL

1903

THE LIFE
AND WORK
OF

ALFRED GILBERT.

R.A., M.V.O., D.C.L.

By

Joseph Hatton.

Illustrated.

THE EASTER NUMBER
OF ART THE
JOURNAL

H. VIRTUE & CO., LTD.

LONDON: SIMPKIN, MARSHALL, HAMILTON, KENT & CO., LTD.

Artists can always take some steps to ensuring their own posterity, and the proper representation of their work. Many keep their own records, inventories of when pieces are sold, and where they go. Nowadays it is easy to keep copious photographic records of every piece, and almost every professional sculptor has some printed material with colour reproductions. In the 19th century the options were more limited, and relatively more expensive. However, a sculptor such as Count Gleichen, one of the Royal Family, was well able to afford to have compiled a bound album of photographs of his works. Calder Marshall's album of photographs shows not only individual works, like Gleichen's, but also provides tantalising glimpses of the sculptor's studio, seemingly frozen in time.

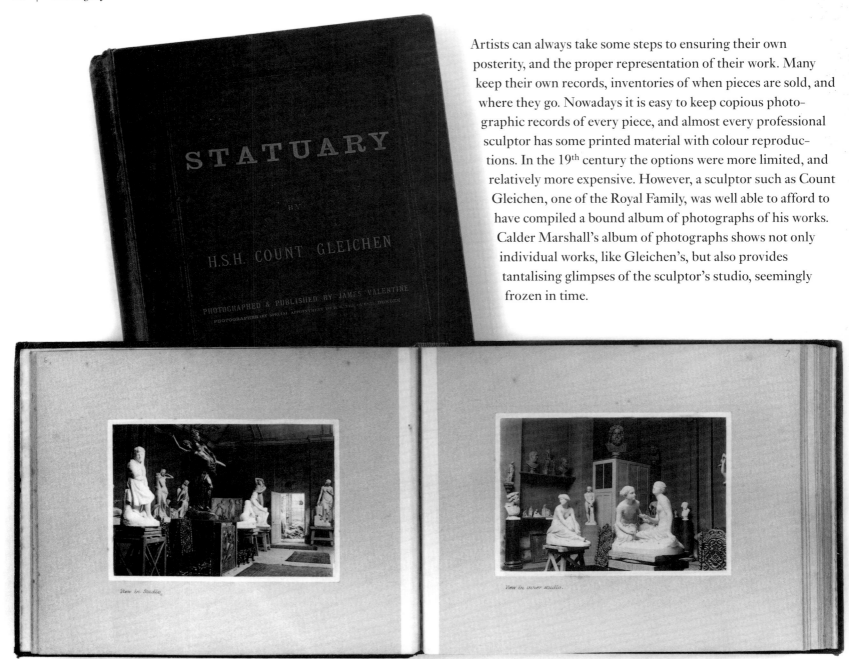

Album of photographs of works by HSH **Count Gleichen** photographed and published by James Valentine, *c.* 1890s. 290 × 230 mm. Album with photographs of sculptures by **William Calder Marshall** from photographs by his son printed by H. T. Malby n.d. 271 × 223 mm

Opposite

After an artist's death, the family have to consider how to deal with the work, the studio, and the reputation. In the case of the sculptor, this is always more difficult, given the bulk and weight of most sculpture. After recording the artist's works and workplace in photography, a selling exhibition may well be an effective way of commemorating the artist and of selling on works while the reputation is high, or of clearing out the studio. Though these catalogues from posthumous sales are in themselves modest, they may record events that were rather more lavish. Nevertheless, they are poignant reminders of what is left at the end of a working life, while hinting at the many layers of experience which lie behind these simple lists of titles. It is those layers – the facets of a sculptor's working life – which this book has aimed to highlight and which can be studied in depth, and for real, in the archive itself.

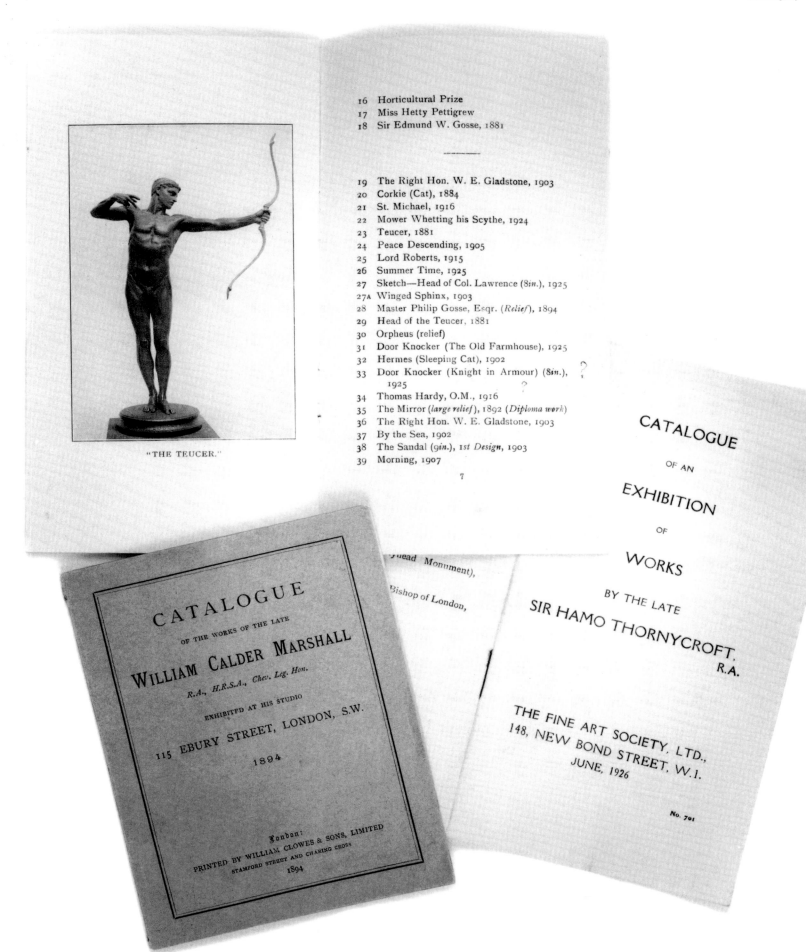

"THE TEUCER."

16 Horticultural Prize
17 Miss Hetty Pettigrew
18 Sir Edmund W. Gosse, 1881

———————

19 The Right Hon. W. E. Gladstone, 1903
20 Corkie (Cat), 1884
21 St. Michael, 1916
22 Mower Whetting his Scythe, 1924
23 Teucer, 1881
24 Peace Descending, 1905
25 Lord Roberts, 1915
26 Summer Time, 1925
27 Sketch—Head of Col. Lawrence (8*in.*), 1925
27A Winged Sphinx, 1903
28 Master Philip Gosse, Esqr. (*Relief*), 1894
29 Head of the Teucer, 1881
30 Orpheus (relief)
31 Door Knocker (The Old Farmhouse), 1925
32 Hermes (Sleeping Cat), 1902
33 Door Knocker (Knight in Armour) (8*in.*), 1925
34 Thomas Hardy, O.M., 1916
35 The Mirror (*large relief*), 1892 (*Diploma work*)
36 The Right Hon. W. E. Gladstone, 1903
37 By the Sea, 1902
38 The Sandal (9*in.*), 1st *Design*, 1903
39 Morning, 1907

7

CATALOGUE OF AN EXHIBITION OF WORKS BY THE LATE SIR HAMO THORNYCROFT, R.A.

THE FINE ART SOCIETY, LTD., 148, NEW BOND STREET, W.1. JUNE, 1926

No. 701

CATALOGUE OF THE WORKS OF THE LATE WILLIAM CALDER MARSHALL R.A., H.R.S.A., Chev. Leg. Hon. EXHIBITED AT HIS STUDIO 115 EBURY STREET, LONDON, S.W. 1894

London: PRINTED BY WILLIAM CLOWES & SONS, LIMITED STAMFORD STREET AND CHARING CROSS 1894

Two posthumous catalogues of an exhibition of Sir Hamo Thornycroft's work, 1926. 183 × 100 mm. Posthumous catalogue for an exhibition of William Calder Marshall's work, 1894. 136 × 107 mm

Centre for the Study of Sculpture
Concise Listing of the Archive

The content of each separate archive is briefly described below and is followed by a short paragraph of key information concerning the artist. If the material consists of separate drawings the size of the drawing is usually mentioned. In many cases a more detailed list of a given holding is available on request.

Armstead, Henry Hugh; 1828–1905; Drawing of a standing male figure. Size: 720 × 440 mm. Collection of 32 mounted photographs showing a cross section of his work including memorials, plaques and statues/monuments. Acquired in 1992. Two deeds of inauguration making Armstead an associate member and full member respectively of the Royal Academy (1875 & 1879). Size: 663 × 504 mm. Acquired in 1992.

Henry Hugh Armstead was born and died in London. He was a sculptor, silversmith and illustrator. He attended the Royal Academy Schools and exhibited many busts and reliefs at the Royal Academy (R.A.) (1851–1904). After he failed to gain recognition for his silver 'Outram Shield' (exhibited R.A. 1862) he turned his attention to sculpture and worked in collaboration with architects, e.g. on the decorations for the 'Colonial Office'. He designed half of the podium frieze for the 'Albert Memorial' (1863–72) in Kensington Gardens. The 'Painters', 'Poets' and 'Musicians' and bronze statues of 'Medicine', 'Rhetoric', 'Chemistry' and 'Astronomy' for this memorial are represented in the Centre's archive as are his major works 'David and the Lion' and 'Lieutenant Waghorn'. Armstead's naturalistic approach, and the variety of media he used, made him a forerunner of the New Sculpture movement.

Bacon, John; 1740–1799; Preparatory sketch for a funerary monument (n.d.). Size: 166 × 213 mm. Acquired in 1991.

John Bacon was born and died in London. He was apprenticed to the Lambeth porcelain works as a modeller and worked from 1769 onwards for Coade's Artificial Stone Manufactory. He started studying at the Royal Academy in 1769 and won the first gold medal ever to be presented there. Alongside his prolific work as a ceramicist, he produced a number of bronze sculptures, the figures of 'Hercules and Atlas' (1784) at the Oxford Observatory and the ornamental clockcase at Buckingham Palace showing the figures of 'Vigilance and Patience' (1789). He executed monuments for Bristol Cathedral, Westminster Abbey and St Paul's Cathedral, exhibited at the Free Society (1762–1764) and at the Royal Academy (1769–1799).

Bailey, Edward Hodges; 1788–1867; Several sketches of two winged figures, possibly a design for a plaque (n.d.). Size: 246 × 344 mm, when folded. Acquired in 1996.

Edward Hodges Bailey was born in Bristol and died in London. He made two groups after Flaxman which caught Flaxman's attention. He thereafter became Flaxman's pupil and a student at the Royal Academy. He is now remembered for his public sculpture, his 'Earl Grey' (1837) and the 'Statue of Nelson' (1843) in Trafalgar Square. He was also an accomplished portrait sculptor.

Bell, Quentin; b.1910; 3 Drawings relating to the site of the Leeds University figure 'The Dreamer', 7 sheets of drawings of this figure and technical drawings showing how the figure was to be fixed, 1 photocopy. 'The Dreamer' was unveiled in 1982. Donated in 1982.

Quentin Bell was the son of the writer Clive Bell. He studied pottery in Staffordshire and sculpture in Rome. He wrote many books, among which a biography of Virginia Woolf. He was Professor of Fine Arts at Leeds University (1962–7), Slade Professor at Oxford and Professor at Sussex University.

Bradshaw, Laurence; 1899–1978; Ringbinder with correspondence, accounts, agreements and sketches (1935–74), 31 drawings (1935–57), 20 loose photographs (1926–57), ringbinder with 42 photographs (1927–58 & 1989), ringbinder with 35 photographs (1940s–1970), typescripts of articles relating to: 'Ideas on Art and Artists', the decay of the Epstein figures on Rhodesia House, and the Karl Marx monument; 3 newspaper cutting books (1917–83), some loose newspaper cuttings (1935–91), folder with newspaper cuttings (1955–86), various postcards, appeal fund leaflet and invitation card to the Karl Marx monument. Donated by Mrs Eileen Bradshaw in 1994. There have been a number of small additions to the archive up to August 1995, including the Karl Marx Memorial maquette.

Laurence Henderson Bradshaw was born in Wallasey on Merseyside and died in London. He was a sculptor, engraver and painter. Bradshaw was educated at Liverpool University and Art School. He turned to sculpture in the 1920s. Bradshaw was involved with the British Soviet Friendship Society, the Royal Society of British Sculptors, and was elected Master of the Art Workers Guild in 1958. He was the official war artist for the Norwegian government in World War II and was rewarded, for his contribution to the arts, with a civil list pension from the British government. His first major commission was a six panel piece depicting the life of St Philip Neri and banners for the Brompton Oratory (positioned in London, 1928). He carried out many more public commissions, particularly in conjunction with architects e.g. Mother and Child (*c.* 1935) on the Radcliffe Maternity Home, as well as many portrait busts. Bradshaw's best known, but also most controversial work, is the Karl Marx Memorial (1956) in Highgate Cemetery. It is this memorial which is especially well documented in the archive. His designs for theatre scenery are housed in the Victoria and Albert Museum.

Cawthra, Hermon; 1886–1971; 2 Albums of photographs, 50 loose photographs, newspaper cuttings (1926–39), portfolio of Selfridge's decorations for the Coronation of George VI and Queen Victoria (1937), booklet 'Thoughts on a day of reckoning' (1955). Given to the Centre for the Study of Sculpture by Laurence Davis and the Public Monuments & Sculpture Association in 1995.

Hermon Cawthra received his art training first in Yorkshire and then at the Royal College of Art (1909–11) and Royal Academy Schools (1912–16). He exhibited at the Royal Academy (1912–65) and taught sculpture at Brighton School of Art. Among his works are 'Britannia' (1926), on the Fire Offices at Piccadilly Circus, the four figures of putti with different animals on Leeds Civic Hall (opened by George V in 1933), the 'Robert Burns' statue (unveiled by J. Ramsey MacDonald at St Michael's Churchyard, Dumfries, 1936) and 'Memorial to the Earl of Meath' (1937), Hyde Park.

Chantrey, Francis; 1781–1841; Drawing of the head of the First Duke of Wellington (n.d.). Size: 395 × 302 mm. A bust and statue were made of Wellington in 1837 and 1840. Donated by David Bindman in 1990.

Sir Francis Chantrey was born in Norton, Derbyshire, and died in London. He was apprenticed to a carver and gilder in Sheffield and received lessons in drawing from Raphael Smith. He exhibited work in a Neo-classical style at the Royal Academy from 1804 to his death and became one of Britain's leading portrait sculptors. One of his major works is the equestrian statue of 'George IV' (1828) in Trafalgar Square.

Clarke, Geoffrey; b.1924; Royal College of Art thesis containing original prints bound in leather with decoration (1952). Size: 580 × 393 mm. Bought in 1995.

Geoffrey Clarke was born in Darley Dale, Derbyshire. He is a sculptor in metal, etcher and a designer of stained glass. He studied at Preston School of Art (1940–1), Manchester School of Art (1941–2), Lancaster and Morecambe School of Arts and Crafts (1947–8) and the Royal College of Art (1948–52). He became celebrated as a sculptor in iron in the 1950s. His largest and most important project was the Coventry Cathedral commission which involved three windows (1952–6), the 'Flying Cross' (installed by helicopter, 1962) and various other pieces. He also executed an iron sculpture for the 'Time Life Building' (1952), 'Extraction and Refining of Oil' (1959), along with many sculptures for British universities. He taught at Colchester and was head of the Light Transmission and Projection Department at the Royal College of Art (1968–73).

Cox, Stephen (Joseph); b.1946; Two small sketchbooks (1983 & 1985). Size: 146 × 203 and 114 × 178 mm. Acquired in 1988. 14 Live pigment pieces of various sizes (n.d.). Donated in 1994.

5 Numbered drawings various sizes (1979). Acquired in 1995. (2 Audio cassettes with commentaries on the above mentioned sketchbooks and 2 Tate Gallery lectures are also available for research).

Stephen Cox was born in Bristol. He attended the West of England College of Art (1964–5), Loughborough College of Art (1965–6) and later Central School of Art and Design (1966–1968). He taught at Coventry College of Art (1968–72) and various other colleges (1975–1981, part-time) and Bristol Central School of Art & Design (1995 till present). From the 1980s Cox was influenced by Italian and Indian traditions and materials. In 1986 he established a studio for stone-carving in India and more recently he has worked with Egyptian granites and carvers.

Cribb, Joseph Herbert; 1892–1967; 50 Letters from Eric Gill to Joseph Cribb, some in Mary Gill's hand but signed by Eric Gill. 4 Letters by Mary Gill, notes made on Cribb's headed notepaper, 12 postcards from Eric Gill to Joseph Cribb and 1 from Mary Gill. The correspondence mainly concerns commissions for lettering and sculpture (1924–31). There are also 2 miscellaneous letters (1926 & 1962). Acquired in 1993.

Joseph Cribb was apprenticed to Eric Gill (1906), and moved to Ditchling with Gill. After the First World War he opened his own workshop but joined the Guild of St Joseph and St Dominic when this was founded in 1921. When Gill moved away from Ditchling after a quarrel in 1924, Joseph Cribb took over the workshop. His works include the inscription on Epstein's monument to Oscar Wilde, the inscription on Epstein's tomb stone (1959) and a memorial plaque for Gill's birthplace.

Epstein, Jacob; 1880–1959; Sketchbook of 87 drawings related to Rima relief on W. H. Hudson memorial (1923–1924). Size: 451 × 587 mm. Acquired in 1983. Some letters, three albums of photographs (c. 1908–39), album with cuttings from *The New Age* – 'War notes' (1915–16), 2 albums of newspaper cuttings relating to 'Adam' (1939), album with newspaper cuttings relating to 'Jacob and the Angel' (1942), **Auguste Rodin's** (1840–1917) business card and letter (1904), various drawings including studies for the 'Maternity' (1910), studies relating to the British Medical Association Building (1907–8), studies for the figures of 'Day' and 'Night' on London Underground Building (1928–9), studies for the 'Bowater House Group' (1957–8), Epstein's copy of 'Fleurs du Mal' by Baudelaire with drawing by Epstein (1904) and c. 510 photographs. Acquired from and donated by Beth Lipkin between 1983 and 1988. 'The Parthenon Frieze as it would have appeared had it been designed by Epstein' – cartoon by Edward Tennyson Reed (n.d.). Acquired in 1988. 14 Letters relating to the bust of George Black (1942–6). Donated in memory of Dr Black in 1990. 'Meum' (Mrs Lindsell-Stewart) sketchbook (1916–18). Size: 302 × 237 mm. Acquired in 1991. (Apart from the archive itself there are many photocopied newspaper cuttings available with early criticism from the press).

Epstein was born in New York to Polish-Jewish parents and died in London. He spent his childhood in America and his talent was recognised by the early 1890s when a prize took him to the Art Students League, where he attended life classes for eight years. He left for Paris in 1902 and was soon admitted to classes at the Ecole des Beaux-Arts. Six months later Epstein moved to the Académie Julian. These years in Paris were interrupted by a brief visit to England in 1904, where he settled in 1905. He worked in Paris on the Oscar Wilde monument (1909–12), and made 'Rockdrill' (1913–15), influenced by the English Vorticists, after his return to Britain. Epstein's reputation for controversy was mainly established through his carving, notably the British Medical Association figures, the monuments to W. H. Hudson and a series of alabaster carvings including 'Adam' and 'Jacob and The Angel'. His work on the London Underground Electric Railways Building, designed by the architect Charles Holden, was better received, while the bulk of his portraiture was much appreciated, e.g. 'Joseph Conrad' (1924) and 'Winston Churchill' (1946). Epstein had a large personal collection of 'primitive' sculpture from which he drew much of his inspiration.

Fisher, John; John and William; 1736–1804, 1760–1839 & 1777–1815; Two indentures of apprenticeship between John & John Fisher and John & William Fisher (1785 & 1787). Presented by Dorothy and Florence Porteous in 1983.

John Fisher the Elder's figures, exhibited at the Free Society of Artists in 1761, were much appreciated by the Marquess of Rockingham. The Marquess commissioned several works from him, e.g. two chimney-pieces. The Marquess persuaded John to move to York. John's son John was taken on as apprentice as was his son William. It is often unclear whose work particular monuments actually were. Among their works are many monuments, a statue of Sir George Savile (1784) and busts of Pitt, Newton and Wellington. William Fisher left the family business and settled in London in 1806. He exhibited in the Royal Academy between 1801 and 1811, e.g. marble bas-relief of greyhounds and various busts.

Flaxman, John; 1755–1826; Sheet of figure studies (c. 1787–94). Size: 117 × 187 mm. Bequeathed by Agnes & Norman Lupton in 1952. Drawing of two muses, probably a design for a chimney piece (n.d.). Size: 217 × 342 mm. Donated anonymously in 1983. 2 Designs of Tympanum for Buckingham Palace (1826). Size: 190 × 245 mm and 190 × 245 mm. Donated in 1983. *Sujets de l'Odissée d'Homère gravés d'après les dessins et compositions de John Flaxman Sculptr Anglais* (1803). Engraving by William Bond after a drawing by Henry Corbould showing the monument to 'Sir John Beckett and William Walker' sculpted by Flaxman. Published by Robinson Son & Holdsworth, Leeds & John Hurst Wakefield (1816). Size: 437 × 270 mm. Acquired in 1987.

John Flaxman was born in York and died in London. His father was a plasterer. His talent was noticed by Romney and Rev Mathew. When he was twelve-years-old he exhibited a model after the antique in the Free Society of Artists and at fifteen he gained a silver medal at the Royal Academy for his wax model 'Neptune'. He entered the Royal Academy in 1770 and started working for Wedgwood in 1775 for whom he later travelled to Rome (1787–1794). His illustrations to the Illiad and the Odyssey are regarded as his best work from this period. He was appointed professor of sculpture at the Royal Academy (1810) and became one of the most repected sculptors of the time.

Fleischmann, Arthur; 1896–1990; 11 Photographs, c22 press cuttings (1950–1 & 1991), souvenir leaflet relating to his 'Mermaid' (Lockheed Fountain) for the Festival of Britain (1951) and *Punch* (1951). Acquired in 1994.

Arthur Fleischmann was born in Bratislava, Slovakia, and died in Spain. He studied medicine in Budapest and Prague before turning towards art. His sculpture training started in Prague (1920) and continued in Vienna (1922) where he was awarded a scholarship to the Master School of Sculpture. He taught in Vienna at the Women's Art Academy in the early 1930s. In the 1930s he travelled to Italy and Paris, lived in South Africa and Bali and went on to live in Australia until he moved to Britain in 1948. From the late 1940s Fleischmann worked in collaboration with the Imperial Chemical Industries (ICI). He developed the use of perspex in sculpture and also specialised in portrait busts. His devotion to the Catholic faith is central to his work: he sculpted four Popes and executed commissions for churches in England and abroad.

Forsyth, James; 1826–1910; Album of contemporary photographs of James Forsyth's work related to architecture in England and Scotland. Inscribed on front cover with 'Jean Mitchell Peatie from her cousin Caroline Robert Mitchell'. The first page shows a watercolour by Forsyth from 1880. Size: 458 × 380 mm. Acquired in 1986.

James Forsyth was born and died in London. He exhibited at the Royal Academy (1864–1889) and specialised in genre and classical statuettes. The album mentioned above shows e.g. his restoration work at Wells Cathedral and the pulpit in Worcester Cathedral.

Frampton, George; 1860–1928; c405 Photographs covering his architectural oeuvre, ideal works and busts but also jewellery, medals and design work. The programme for the unveiling of the 'Queen Victoria' in Leeds (1905). Given to the Centre for the Study of Sculpture by Laurence Davis and the Public Monuments & Sculpture Association in 1995.

George Frampton was born in London and died there. He studied at Lambeth School, the Royal Academy Schools (1881–1887) and in Paris from where he returned in 1889. He promoted the Arts and Crafts Movement and is notable for his fine modelling and sensitive attention to detail. Among his best known works are 'Peter Pan' (1910) in Kensington Gardens and 'Mysteriarch' (1892) in the R.A. Frampton also worked successfully on a number of architectural commissions, the most notable being the Lloyd's Registry of Shipping (1898–1901). He exhibited at the Royal Academy (1884–1904).

Francis, John; 1780–1861; Sketchbook, for more information see Thomas Thornycroft archive.

Galizia and Son Ltd Fine Art Bronze Foundry, John; Four casting ledgers (1930–1965), c538 original foundry photographs, many showing work of Benno Elkan and Robert Glen, and various printed ephemera (1947, 1963, 1971, 1972, 1979, and 1984). Bought in 1992.

The Galizia foundry was started in the 1930s by John Galizia. As the casting ledgers show, in the second half of the 1950s well known sculptors like Frink, Reid Dick, Paolozzi, Armitage, Turnbull, Wheeler, Bradshaw, Fleischmann, Epstein, Wright and McWilliam all made use of the foundry. The ledgers give basic information about dates and payments.

Gilbert, Alfred; 1854–1934; 56 Letters to Douglas Illingworth and 8 small photographs (1911–4, 1918–20, 1923 and 1925). Acquired in 1993. 2 Letters to Farquhar (1894, 1896) and 1 speech sent to the president at the banquet of the International Society of Sculptors, Painters and Gravers (1909).

Alfred Gilbert was born and died in London. He was a medallist, goldsmith and draughtsman as well as sculptor. He was a leading figure in the New Sculpture movement and made his best works when left to his own devices. Gilbert's enthusiasm allowed him sometimes to forget the commercial aspects of his trade, resulting eventually in bankruptcy. He enrolled in Thomas Heatherley's Art School (1872), the Royal Academy Schools (1875–8), Ecole des Beaux-Arts and lived in Italy (1878–1885) but visited London several times during this period. His stay in France and Italy greatly influenced his work. After his return from Italy Gilbert was responsible for popularising the lost-wax casting method in Britain. He executed three major monumental works: the 'Shaftesbury Fountain' with the figure of 'Eros' (1885–93), the jubilee monument to 'Queen Victoria' (1887–1912) and the tomb of 'Prince Albert Victor, Duke of Clarence' (1892–1901 & 1926–8). Gilbert became a full member of the Royal Academy in 1892 and was appointed professor of sculpture in 1900. Then followed a difficult period during which he lived in Belgium, mainly to avoid problems with his unfinished commissions and his creditors, at first returning to London fairly frequently. The speech listed among the archive material is interesting in that it refers to his absence: "That I am not with you, in the flesh, is my misfortune, and not my fault." In 1909 he resigned from the RA under some pressure from articles in the press. In 1925 he went to Italy and finally returned to London in 1926 through mediation from his future biographer, Isabel McAllister and Helen Gleichen. After his return he finished the 'Clarence' tomb and his last important commission, the monument to 'Queen Alexandra' (1926–32).

Gill, Eric; 1882–1940; 145 Photographs including portraits of the artist and his work. Acquired in 1986. 1 Letter from Gill to Douglas (1929), 1 photograph, several prints of alphabets and pages of books. Donated anonymously in 1996.

Eric Gill was born in Brighton, son of an assistant minister, and died in Harefield House Hospital, Middlesex. He was an artist craftsman who made wood engravings, sculptures, drawings, illustrations and typographic work and was a prolific writer. He attended Chichester Technical and Art School (1897), joined Edward Johnston's lettering class at the Central School of Arts and Crafts (1899) and became an apprentice to the architect of the Ecclesiastical Commissioners (1900–3) . Gill and his wife, Ethel Mary Moore, moved to Ditchling in 1907. In 1913 they converted to the Catholic Church. The Craft Guild of St Joseph and St Dominic was formed by the 'Ditchling Community' in 1921 but Gill left it in 1924 after a quarrel. In 1933 Gill was a founder of the Artists' International Association to oppose the rise of Fascism and became involved in speaking and writing for peace. In 1937 he was awarded Honorary Associateship of the Royal Society of British Sculptors and was elected Associate member of the Royal Academy. His largest work was the panel for the League of Nations Building in Geneva. Many of his works were made for religious institutions, one of the first commissions being the 'Stations of the Cross' in Westminster Cathedral (1914–18).

Gleichen, Count Victor; 1833–1891; Album with 77 photographs of Count Gleichen, Admiral Prince Victor of Hohenlohe-Langenburgh, showing a variety of works. Acquired in 1993.

Count Gleichen was born in Langenburg and buried in Ascot; his tombstone sculpted by his daughter. He was the son of Queen Victoria's half-sister. He served in the armed forces but because of ill health was unable to continue this career. In 1866 he became governor and constable of Windsor Castle. He studied under William Theed and set up his own studio in St James's Palace where he made his sculptures and watercolours. It was only later in life that he turned to art as a career, after financial hardship forced him to do so. His most important work was the colossal statue of 'Alfred the Great' in Sicilian marble in the city square of Wantage (1877). Successful busts were: 'Earl of Beaconsfield' (1880), 'Marquis of Salisbury' and 'Sir Harry Keppel' (exhibited in the RA, 1882), whom he had served in the army. He exhibited in the Royal Academy (1868–1892).

Guglielmi, Paolo; (active late 1820s–late 1840s); 5 Drawings after sculptures by Henry Timbell, William Theed and Richard James Wyatt (c. 1835–48). Size: average c. 400 × 290 mm. Acquired in 1993.

Hepworth, Barbara; 1903–1975; 2 Letters (1950), 1 letter relating to the Yorkshire Artists' Exhibition (1953). From Leeds City Art Gallery exhibition files.

Barbara Hepworth was born in Wakefield and died in St Ives. She attended Leeds School of Art in 1919 and the Royal College of Art in London (1920–1923). She participated in the Venice Biennale in 1950 and gained two commissions for the Festival of Britain in 1951. Her first post-war exhibitions were held in Leeds and Halifax, and she retained an allegiance to Yorkshire though based in Cornwall.

Hoskin, John; 1921–1990; c57 Sketches (1950s–1960s and 1983), correspondence relating to three different projects, the competition and later commission for the new Town Hall in Darlington (1969–72), a commission for Provincial Insurance Company (1969–72), an open air exhibition with correspondence between South Western Arts Association and Southern Arts Association (1973), 3 posters (1961 & 1970) and c10 photographs (1950s & 60s). Acquired in 1994.

John Hoskin was born in Cheltenham and died in London. He trained as an architectural draughtsman. His first exhibition was in 1954 (London Group) and his first one-man exhibition was at the Aldeburgh Festival (1956). He participated in numerous Arts Council and British Council Travelling exhibitions and took part in the 7th Tokyo Biennale in 1963. He held various teaching posts during his career, and was head of sculpture at the Bath Academy of Art (1957–67) and head of painting at Winchester School of Art (1978). His commissions included a reredos for St Stephen's Church (1958–9), Bristol, and for Nuffield College Chapel (1960), Oxford.

International Exhibition of 1862; Album of 74 Photographs of the International Exhibition of 1862 which includes some photographs of the Crystal Palace, which had been moved to Sydenham in 1854. Acquired in 1996.

Images included in the photographs are Thorvaldsen's 'Mercury', Harriet Hosmer's rosy tinted 'Zenobia', works by Foley, works by Gibson and many others.

Kidner, Michael; b.1917; 20 Preparatory drawings from his column and lattices series and six photographs (1970, 1972–4, 1984 & 1987). Sizes c. 590 × 844 mm. Acquired from and donated by the artist in 1995. (Taped interview also available for study.)

Michael Kidner was born in Kettering. He read History and Anthropology at Cambridge University (1936–9) and landscape architecture at Ohio State University (1940–1). He went for a very brief period to Goldsmiths' College of Art. It was not until the early 1950s that Kidner seriously began to consider a career in painting. As a result he went to Paris and studied with André Lhôte for about six months. In 1956 he returned to England where he spent six months in St Ives exploring landscape abstraction and in 1957 he moved to London where he was influenced by American Abstract Expressionism via exhibitions at the Tate Gallery. His first one-man exhibition was held at St Hilda's College, Oxford (1959) and many more followed as he enjoyed widespread acclaim in the 1960s. He has been Artist in Residence at both the University of Sussex (1967) and the University of Washington DC (1968) and held teaching posts at Bath Academy of Art (1964–84) and more recently Chelsea School of Art (1981–84).

Koenig, Ghisha; 1921–1993; 11 Large sketchbooks and 8 smaller sketchbooks (late 1940s – early 1980s). Size: average 502 × 354 mm & 260 × 210 mm. Acquired in 1994.

Ghisha Koenig was born and died in London. She gained a scholarship to Hornsey School of Art and after the war she continued her studies at the Chelsea School of Art under Henry Moore (1947–9). She worked in factories around her home in St Mary Cray, Kent, observing people in their workplace and making many drawings before she actually started making her work. She was a modeller rather than a carver, and worked mainly in relief.

Ledward, Gilbert; 1888–1960; 9 Studies and 1 blueprint for 'Guards' Division Memorial' (1922–6). Size: *c.* 370 × 280 mm. Acquired and donated in 1988. *c*162 Photographs covering his different pieces of work and views of the Trenches (1914–18), *c*22 newspaper cuttings (1946 & 1948). Acquired in 1988. Photocopy of typescript autobiography available for study.

Gilbert Ledward was born and died in London. He was a student at the Arts & Crafts School in Langham Place, the Academy in Karlsruhe, the Royal College of Art and the Royal Academy Schools. Whilst at the latter he won the first travel scholarship for sculpture and became the first Rome scholar for Sculpture (1913). His time in Rome influenced his work considerably. He became professor at the Royal College of Art (1927–9), where Henry Moore was his assistant. Ledward founded his own company in 1934 called 'Sculptured Memorials and Headstones', with which various sculptors were associated. In the Second World War the company moved its headquarters out of London to Eric Gill's home in Buckinghamshire. Many of Ledward's public commissions were war memorials of which the 'Guards' Division Memorial' in St James's Park is the best known; the guardsmen on the memorial were made of melted down German guns. The memorial was damaged in the Second World War and some of the damage was left as a reminder. Other important works were 'Memorial to the Missing' at Ploegsteert in Belgium (1926–9), the 'Memorial to the Submarine Service, Commandos and Airbourne Forces' (1947, unveiled 1948 in the cloister of Westminster Abbey) and the 'Venus Fountain' (1953).

Marshall, William Calder; 1813–1894; Album with 43 photographs photographed by Charles J. Marshall, son of William (1850s). Catalogue of posthumous exhibition of his works at his studio in Ebury St London (1894). Acquired in 1992.

William Calder Marshall was born in Edinburgh and died in London. He was educated at the Edinburgh Academy, the Royal Academy Schools (1834) and studied in the studios of Chantrey and Bailey. After visiting Rome (1836–1838) he settled in London (1839). He exhibited in the Royal Scottish Academy (1833–1926 posthumous) and in the Royal Academy (1835–1891). He made the statues of the 'Lord Clarendon' and 'Lord Somers' (1852 & 1855) and 'Agriculture' on the Albert Memorial (1863–72).

Mestrovic, Ivan; 1883–1962; 9 Photographs of sculptures (1910, 1917 & n.d.).

Ivan Mestrovic was born in Vrpolje, Slovenia, and died in South Bend, Indiana. He was trained as a stone-carver. He studied at the Vienna Academy (1899–1904) and trained further in Paris (1907–9) and Rome (1911–14). The First World War caused him to move to London where he had a major exhibition in the Victoria & Albert Museum. After the war he moved to Geneva (1916) and later to Zagreb (1919) where he became lecturer and later head of the Academy. The Second World War again unsettled his life, and after a period of imprisonment he left Zagreb and took up a professorship in America where he became an American citizen (1954). In his London period he made pieces for churches and portrait busts.

Meyrick, George; b.1953; 20 Leaves of a sketchbook for 'Untitled (Terracotta)' (1984). Acquired in 1984.

George Meyrick was born in London. He studied at St Martin's School of Art (1971–72), Brighton Polytechnic (1972–75) and Chelsea School of Art (1975–76). His first group exhibition was in a touring show, 'Six Young British Sculptors' (1978), and his first one-man exhibition at S. East Gallery (London 1981).

Monchaux, de, Cathy; b.1960; 6 Preparatory drawings (1992–4). Size: smallest 457 × 447 mm & largest 1020 × 910 mm. Acquired in 1994.

Cathy de Monchaux was born in London. She studied at the Camberwell School of Art (1980–83) and Goldsmiths' College (1983–87). She does not exhibit her drawings, which are strictly working sketches. Their linearity, interest in pattern-making and symmetry closely reflect her finished sculpture.

Moore, Henry; 1898–1986; Lecture notes 'History of Sculpture' and 10 pages of notes on architecture (1920), 3 letters to Jocelyn Horner (1923), and typescript of the play 'Narayana and Bhataryan (*c.* 1920). Bequeathed by the late Jocelyn Horner to the LACF in memory of Ernest Musgrave in 1993. Programme for 'Narayana and Bhataryan'. Acquired in 1982. 11 Letters to Mr Philip Hendy (1938–52), and 8 carbon copies of letters from Philip Hendy to Henry Moore (1944 & 1952). From Leeds City Art Gallery files. Dinner menu for event in Leeds Civic Hall with message from Henry Moore (1979). Cover of *Poetry* showing Henry Moore's 'The Lyre Bird' and a different version of the same theme (1942). (Apart from the archive itself there are many photocopied newspaper cuttings available with early criticism from the press).

Henry Moore was born in Castleford and died in Perry Green. He went to Leeds School of Art in 1919 and was awarded a scholarship to attend the Royal College of Art in 1921. His first public commission was to make one of the 'Winds' for the London Underground building (1928–9) in a programme led by Gill. He was appointed sculpture instructor at the Royal College (1924) and had his first one-man exhibition in the Warren Gallery (1928). When the Second World War broke out he moved to Hertfordshire. His appointment as an official war artist and his shelter drawings from this period brought him widespread popularity, and after showing at the Venice Biennale in 1948 he went on to become one of the most successful sculptors ever.

Nash, David; b.1945; 34 Letters and faxes between David Nash and the curator and assistant curator of the Centre of Contemporary Art (Ujazdowski Castle, Poland), the British Council and the Annely Juda Gallery, press releases, plans of exhibition spaces, a sheet planning his travels abroad, 1 sketchbook, 3 drawings, 38 photographs, photocopies of part of his diary, catalogue dummies and the final version of the catalogue from the 1991 project in Poland (1990–2). Donated in 1996.

David Nash was born in Esher, Surrey. He went to Kingston College of Art (1963), Brighton College (1964–7) and Chelsea School of Art (1969–70). His first one-man show was at the York Festival (1973). Since 1967 he has lived in Blaenau Ffestiniog in the North of Wales where he has several ongoing projects, including sculptures made with living trees. He has exhibited widely in many countries around the world including the USA and Japan.

Nollekens, Joseph, Studio; 1737–1823; Drawing of the figure of 'Ocean' appearing on the monument to 'Captains Bayne, Blair and Lord Manners' (n.d.). Size: 245 × 276 mm. Acquired in 1986.

Joseph Nollekens was born and died in London. He was apprenticed to Peter Scheemakers in 1750. He lived in Rome (1762–1770) where he made copies from the antique which he sold to Englishmen on their Grand Tour. He made many funerary monuments and portrait busts.

Peskett, Eric; b.1914; 7 Drawings, each showing a different plant form, e.g. a horse chestnut, two onions, a withered daffodil, an orchid blossom etc (1981–92). Size: various, between 660 × 510 & 566 × 763 mm. Ministry of Education exam papers in art and design (late 1950s–early 1960s). Donated in 1995. (A taped interview is available for study).

Eric Peskett was born in Guildford. He attended Brighton School of Art and went on to the Royal College of Art Sculpture School (1935). After the war he continued the travelling scholarship he had to interrupt because of the war. Many of his commissions were architecture related. Peskett taught at Bromley School of Art which later became Ravensbourne College of Art and Design. Peskett divided his professional life between teaching and architectural sculpture, but always reserved time for his more private study of plants and flowers, which he carried through in drawings and wood carvings.

Peri, Peter (Laszlo); 1899–1967; *c*324 Drawings and copies of *c*248 photographs (*c.* second half 1920s–1960s). Acquired in 1995.

Peter Peri was born in Budapest, the eldest son of a large Jewish family, and died in London. He was originally called Ladislas Weisz. (The name Laszlo is short for Ladislas). When he was a teenager he changed his surname to Peri. He made one more name change when he became a naturalised British citizen in 1939, and took Peter as his first name, which might have been his second name in Hungary. Peri started his career in Hungary in a lawyers' office. He subsequently became apprenticed to a stone-carver. He travelled through Czechoslovakia and Austria with a theatre group, eventually settling in Paris, but was expelled from France in 1920 because of subversive activities. He went to live in Berlin where he resumed his sculpture activities and became involved with the 'Sturm' group. His early work is strongly related to Constructivism. He attempted a career in architecture but had to return to his sculptural work. After the Nazis came to power he left Germany and settled in Hampstead. An important exhibition was *London life in concrete*, 1938. He experimented with vertical sculpture from the second half of the 1930s onwards. His 'Little people', which he mainly made from the 1940s into the 1950s, are also significant. In the 1950s he gained some commissions for schools, especially in the Leicestershire area. It was also at this time that he started to work with polyester resin and fibreglass. Examples of his work are 'The Sunbathers', which was on Station Gate of the Royal Festival Hall during the Festival of Britain (1951), 'Two Children Calling a Dog' (1956), Earl Shilton Grammar School (1956) and 'The Coventry Sculpture' (1960) owned by the Herbert Museum and Art Gallery.

Quellinus, Artus I; 1609–1668; 1 Album containing 43 etchings of marble sculpture produced by Hubertus Quellinus (1619[?]–1687). On loan.

Artus Quellinus was born in Antwerp and died there. He was first taught by his father and was then further educated in Italy from where he returned in 1639. He seemed to have spent the remainder of his life travelling for business between Antwerp and Amsterdam but probably also travelled to France and Sweden. Between 1650 and 1664 he worked on the adornment of the Town Hall in Amsterdam with various other sculptors.

Roberts-Jones, Ivor; b.1913; Dossier on the bronze statute of 'Field-Marshall Viscount Slim' (1987–90). The dossier contains some correspondence and notes about the competition and the selection, architect's plan of the site, appeal, invitation to and order of the unveiling ceremony, 3 newspaper cuttings and 37 photographs of the unveiling. Acquired 1996.

Ivor Robert-Jones was born in Oswestry, Shropshire. He attended Goldsmiths' College of Art and the Royal Academy Schools. He had one-man shows at the Beaux Arts Gallery (1957) and the Welsh Arts Council Gallery, Oriel, Cardiff (1978). Major public commissions are 'Winston Churchill' (1973), 'Field Marshall Viscount Slim' (1990) and 'Field Marshall Lord Alanbrooke' (1993).

Thornycroft, Hamo; 1850–1925; The Hamo Thornycroft archive is, together with the Thomas Thornycroft archive, the largest single holding in the Centre. It consists of *c.* 5610 items. There are *c.* 2286 letters, 13 journals (1862–1925), 36 diaries (1886–1925), 32 sketchbooks (1861–1921), 186 drawings, 210 photographs, 4 financial and 10 legal documents, 12 engravings and etchings, 15 poems and prayers, 37 notes and memoranda, 13 lecture notes and speeches, 27 lists, 19 maps, 180 printed ephemera. Donated by Mrs Elfrida Manning in 1982. 1080 Letters, 126 drawings, 522 photographs, 13 poems and prayers, 162 notes & memoranda, 4 maps, 252 printed ephemera. Bequeathed by the late Mrs Elfrida Manning in 1987. 22 Letters and 1 card by Hamo Thornycroft to Theodore Blake Wirgman (1846–1925) mainly about possible rendez-vous (1878–1914). Acquired in 1996.

Hamo was born in London and died in Oxford. He was the youngest son of Mary and Thomas Thornycroft, both sculptors and represented in the Thomas Thornycroft archive. He was the youngest of the six surviving children, two of whom were sculptor-painters, one a painter and one a sculptor. Hamo had the most successful career. He entered the Royal Academy Antique School in 1869 and the Life School in 1870. In this year he helped his father with his work the 'Boadicea' and gained his first commission, a bust. The following year he visited Paris and Rome with two of his sisters. He was an active member of the Royal Academy where he taught (1882–1914) and exhibited from 1872 onwards. His most appreciated piece is 'The Mower' (1884), while other important pieces are 'Teucer' (1882), 'The Sower' (1886), 'General Gordon'

(1888) and the Institute of Chartered Accountants Building (1889–93). The archive includes sketches of realised sculpture but also ones made on holidays. Detailed studies and large size drawings are available for the Institute of Chartered Accountants Building (1889–1893). Thornycroft's sketchbooks were often used to keep accounts and the wages of his models and assistants are recorded in them. Newspaper cuttings and printed ephemera are a very useful starting point for research. Notes used by Elfrida Manning in writing her book *Marble and Bronze* are also held at the Centre. The greatest value of the holding lies in its completeness and scope, (together with the Thomas Thornycroft archive). The archive features a wide variety of people, including the painters Theodore Blake Wirgman and Lawrence Alma Tadema, the writers Edmund Gosse and Siegfried Sassoon, and the artists Armstead and Frederick Leighton, whom he regularly met at the Royal Academy.

Thornycroft, Thomas; 1815–1885; **John Francis** (1780–1861); **Mary Francis** (1814–1895). 185 Letters, 8 drawings by several different members of the family, 9 legal and 2 financial documents, and various miscellaneous items. Donated by the Thornycroft family in 1986. 46 Letters, 1 legal and 1 financial document. Bequest by the late Elfrida Manning in 1987. For more information see Hamo Thornycroft archive.

The first sculptor represented in the extensive Thornycroft archive is John Francis. He was born in Lincolnshire and died in London. He exhibited in the Royal Academy (1820–1857). He was fortunate to be considered a Whig and favourite of William IV which gained him many commissions. Thomas received a commission from Queen Victoria in 1844 for a bust of HRH Prince Albert, of whom he had already executed a bust in 1841 for the Duke of Sussex. He received a commission from HRH Prince Albert to make a sculpture of his favourite greyhound (1848). Those commissions were consolidated by the numerous royal commissions Mary, daughter of John Francis, received from Queen Victoria. Mary's first commission came in 1844. Mary Francis was born in Thornham, Norfolk, and she died in London. In 1840 she married one of her father's pupils, Thomas Thornycroft. He was born in Cheshire and died in London. His benefactor was W. B. Dickenson, who paid for most of his apprenticeship. Many of the surviving letters in the Thomas Thornycroft archive are by Dickenson, who remained a lifelong advisor. Mary and Thomas visited Rome in 1842–3 and met Thorvaldsen and Gibson. They both exhibited regularly in the Royal Academy as well as at the British Institute and both were represented at the Great Exhibition of 1851. Thomas's 'Boadicea' involved a great deal of labour and eventually Mary and Hamo finished it after his death.

Vézelay, Paule; 1892–1984; 11 Photographs (1934–5), 5 cards with correspondence (1960s & 1970), 4 exhibition catalogues and leaflets (1968, and posthumous 1988 & 1993), 7 private view cards (1950s, 1960s & posthumous 1986) and 2 periodicals (1949 & 1969). Partly donated by Mrs Sally Jarman in 1994 & 1995 and partly acquired in 1995. (Transcriptions of 61 letters and cards are available for study covering the years 1936–43, 1945, 1948–9, 1951–2, 1954–9, 1961, 1963–7 & 1974).

Marjorie Agnes Watson-Williams was born in Clifton, Bristol. She changed her name to Paule Vézelay in 1926 shortly after her arrival in Paris where she settled. Her first one-woman exhibition was in Brussels (1920). It was in 1928 that Vézelay created her first purely abstract work. She met **Hans Arp** and his wife Sophie Taeuber in 1933 and was greatly influenced by their work. Vézelay mainly made reliefs, but between 1935–6 she worked on white plaster sculptures, which probably indicates the influential relationship with Arp. In 1938 Vézelay exhibited with Arp, Taeuber-Arp, Domela, Kandinsky, Magnelli and Seligmann in Milan. Two months after the outbreak of war Vézelay moved back to England. She made a post-war visit to Paris in 1946 but did not stay there, deciding instead to return to England. The archive material shows the lifelong friendship between Vézelay and Arp and his wife Sophie and his second wife Marguerite. (Arp had married Marguerite Hagenbach, devoted friend and collector, in 1959. Sophie had died in 1943). Hans Arp died in Basle in 1966.

Vries, Auke, de; b.1939; Four drawings for sculpture at the Christelijke Hogeschool Leeuwarden (1993). Size: *c.* 300 × 560 mm. Donated in 1996.

Auke de Vries was born in Bergum, the Netherlands, and educated as an engineer. He received no formal art education. He started as a painter and made etchings before he made his first sculptures. He has now become known for his linear monumental and architectural works. From 1970 onwards he has held various teaching posts. His best known works are 'Het Maasbeeld' (1982), and pieces for The Netherlands Architectural Institute (1994), Parc Litoral (1992) and Kreuzung Stern (1992).

Westmacott, James Sherwood; 1823–1888; Album of 33 drawings for sculpture (*c*1800–1830). Size: 517 × 520 mm. Acquired in 1992. Drawing of 'The Progress of Navigation and Commerce' (on paper with 1824 watermark). Size: 440 × 560 mm. Acquired in 1989.

James Sherwood Westmacott was a member of a well known family of sculptors of funerary monuments and chimney-pieces and the nephew of Richard Westmacott. He exhibited portrait sculpture in the Royal Academy (1846–1885).

Wilton, Joseph; 1722–1803; Detail of the decoration of S. Ignazio, Rome (*c.* 1852–5). Size: 155 × 240 mm. Design for or study of a monument (*c.* 1852–5). Size: 270 × 123 mm. Designs for or studies of a monument (*c.* 1852–5). Size: 283 × 120 mm and 281 × 118 mm. Acquired in 1975.

Joseph Wilton was born and died in London. He was the son of a plasterer. He studied in Flanders and Paris and later travelled to Italy where he made copies from antique sculptures. In 1755 he returned to Britain. He specialised in chimney-pieces and decorative work.

Wood (of Bristol), Henry; working between 1801–1830; Album of 222 designs for church monuments and some loose drawings of chimney-pieces, mostly by Wood. Joseph Nollekens, Michael Rysbrack and Thomas Paty are also represented. Size: 560 × 445 mm. Acquired in 1984.

Woodington, William Frederick; 1806–1893;
Album of *c*40 drawings (*c*1832).
Size: 353 × 256 mm. Acquired in 1990.

William Frederick Woodington was born in Sutton Coldfield and died in London. He was a sculptor and a painter. He exhibited in the Royal Academy (1825–1882). The Pediment for the Exchange, Liverpool, was exhibited there in 1874.

Woolner, Thomas; 1825–1892; 170 Original studio photographs. Acquired in 1992. 2 Diaries (1864 & 1874). Acquired in 1990.

Thomas Woolner was born in Hadleigh and died in London. He was taught at an early age by William Behnes and furthered his studies in the Royal Academy in 1842 whilst still working for Behnes. He was accepted into the Pre-Raphaelite Brotherhood in 1848. He emigrated to Australia hoping for a better future for himself but returned to Britain in 1854 somewhat disillusioned. After his return his career finally took off. Most of his works were portrait busts, although he also gained commissions for portrait statues, some of which were exported to the colonies. Among his best known works are the 'John Robert Godley' statue (1865) and 'Deaf and Dumb' (exhibited in the 1862 London International Exhibition). His last work was 'The Housemaid' (1892).

Wright, Austin; 1911–1997; 16 Drawings (1958–74). Size: largest 500 × 680 mm, smallest 208 × 330 mm. Acquired in 1995.
34 Sketchbooks, 2 notebooks, 106 photographs and 365 postcards used as sources of inspiration, newspaper cuttings, catalogues and accounts (late 1940s–1994). Donated by Mrs Susan Wright in 1995 and 1996. (Also available for study are Sarah Davenport's 1992 cataloguing notes.)

Austin Wright was born in Chester and died in York. He grew up in Cardiff and studied modern languages in Oxford. He trained to be a teacher and taught French, German and Maths. Although not originally from Yorkshire he spent most of his life there. In 1945 he married and settled in Upper Poppleton, near York. Having started as a teacher, Wright was later able to become a full-time sculptor. The Acquisition Prize at the São Paolo Biennale in 1957 was a great stimulus. He became a Gregory Fellow at the University of Leeds (1961 – 1964) and received an Honorary Doctorate from the University of York (1977). Daily observation of nature fed into his drawings and structural linear aluminium sculptures.

MISCELLANEOUS

Canova, Antonio; 1757–1822; Museum pass signed by Canova admitting Mr Brockedon, Englishman, to the Capitoline Museum (1821). Size: 150 × 240 mm. Acquired in 1983.

Antonio Canova was born in Possagno, near Venice, and died in Venice. From 1781 he was based in Rome, where he became one of the best known neo-classical sculptors.

Hamilton; 1 Letter to William Smith, at the Foreign Office, about the purchase by parliament of the Elgin marbles (1811).

IMPORTANT SECONDARY SOURCES

Dalwood, Hubert; 1924–1976; *c*60 Copies of photographs from his early figurative work to later commissions and large-scale installations.

Hubert Dalwood was born in Bristol and died in London. He studied at Bath Academy of Art (1946–9). He won an Italian Government Scholarship (1951) and after his return he taught at various colleges including Leeds College of Art, Royal College of Art, Hornsey College of Art and Central School of Art (1974–6). His first one-man show was held at Gimpels Fils (1954). He gained various public commissions, many from universities, and had a particular association with the University of Leeds, where he was a Gregory Fellow.

Esdaile, Katherine; A dictionary of sculptors; (those working before 1841 are included, even if the bulk of their work is made later).
Vol.1 Abbot-Cheverton, 2 Chilton-Hartley, 3 Hartshorne-Maxwell, 4 May-Sharman, 5 Sharnhale-Yevele. This holding comprises preparatory material, press cuttings and correspondence.

Goldsworthy, Andy; b1956; Press cuttings, reviews and articles, postcards, catalogues and also photocopies of 18 sketchbooks (1981–8).

Andy Goldsworthy was born in Cheshire and brought up in Yorkshire. He studied at Bradford Art College (1974–5) and Preston Polytechnic (1975–8). He has become known for his work in the open-air, with materials found around him (rocks, leaves, earth, ice and snow). Because of their ephemeral character, the works are documented with photographs, drawings and notes.

Gunnis, Rupert; 9 Volumes of notes additional to the Rupert Gunnis *Dictionary of British Sculptors 1660–1851* (1968). Vol. 1 Abbot-Bird, 2 Bird-Chantry, 3 Chapling-Fisher, 4 Fisher-Ireson, 5 Isbell-Morley, 6 Morris-Rathbone, 7 Rawlings-Spencer, 8 Spill-Wearing, 9 Webb-Young. Research notes, letters and later additions by John Physick.

Illustrated London News; 89 Photographed sheets reproducing articles on sculpture, includes list (1842–1990).

Illustrated magazines, catalogues and journals; *Academy Notes* (1880, 1883,1889), *Academy sketches* (1885), *Royal Academy Pictures* (1892), List of Academicians from 1769–1925 (1925), Royal Academy Catalogues (1926–7, 1929), *The Art Journal* (1882, 1888, 1899), *The Magazine of Art* (1882–3, 1896, 1904), *Artists at Home* (1884), *Pall Mall Gazette 'Extra'* (1884, 1886, 1888, 1889), *The Portfolio* (1888), *Exposition Internationale*, Paris(1889), *The Sculptor Journal* (1898), *The Studio Magazine* (1898, 1911), *The Architectural Review* (1903) and some miscellaneous material. The material is part of the Hamo Thornycroft archive; some of the books formerly owned by Thornycroft are also kept in the Centre's library.

Public sculpture in Leeds; Some of Melanie Hall's extensive research was published in *Leeds Statues Trail* in the *Walk about Series*, (Leeds Civic Trust & Leeds City Council 1995). Her research files contain much more information, gathered over several years, about public sculpture in Leeds and its environs. Four unique photographs from the research files are: F. W. Pomeroy's 'Ralph Thoresby'; Henry Charles Fehr's 'John Harrison'; Alfred Drury's 'Joseph Priestley' and Quentin Bell in his studio with 'The Dreamer'.

Lyons, Mike; b.1943; Polaroid photographs of the sculptor's oeuvre for the unpublished catalogue by Stan Whatmore (1991–4).

PUBLISHED MATERIAL

The library contains a broad range of reference literature and unpublished material (including student dissertations and theses) which relates to the archive. A full bibliography can be supplied on request.

Curtis, Penelope & Terry Friedman eds.
Leeds' Sculpture Collections Illustrated Concise Catalogue (The Centre for the Study of Sculpture, The Henry Moore Institute 1996)

Terry Friedman
Four centuries of Sculptors' Drawings from the Collection of Leeds City Art Galleries (The Henry Moore Centre for the Study of Sculpture 1993)

Friedman, Terry
The Alliance of Sculpture and Architecture: Hamo Thornycroft, John Belcher and the Institute of Chartered Accountants building, (The Henry Moore Centre for the Study of Sculpture, Leeds City Art Galleries 1993)

Terry Friedman
Epstein's Rima, 'The Hyde Park Atrocity': Creation and Controversy (The Henry Moore Centre for the Study of Sculpture 1988)

White, Adam
Hamo Thornycroft & The Martyr General, (The Henry Moore Centre for the Study of Sculpture, Leeds City Art Galleries 1991).

The Sculpture Business
Documents from the Archive

An illustrated handbook and
concise inventory as at January 1997
of the Archive of the
Centre for the Study of Sculpture
at the Henry Moore Institute

Compiled and edited by
Penelope Curtis

Archive listings
Adeline van Roon

The organisation of the archive has benefited
from years of loyal help from volunteers,
among whom we should particularly like to thank
Betty MacAlister and Helen Upton

Published in Great Britain by
The Centre for the Study of Sculpture
The Henry Moore Institute
74 The Headrow
Leeds LS1 3AA

Design/production
Groundwork, Skipton

Photography
Richard Littlewood, Huddersfield

Scanning/reproduction
Leeds Photo Litho

Printed in England by
Steffprint, Keighley

ISBN 1 900081 36 9

Front cover, clockwise from top:
a drawing by **Cathy de Monchaux** (*c.* 1993),
competition rules from the archive of
John Hoskin (1969), a photograph of **Paule Vézelay**
in her studio in Paris (*c.* 1935), a drawing by
John Hoskin (1950s), **Stephen Cox's** sketchbook
(1983), **Jacob Epstein's** measuring calipers
and spectacles, and a 19th-century
stereographic photograph

Inside covers:
Letters to **Thomas Thornycroft** from his patron,
W. B. Dickenson (1835 & *c.* 1837). Dickenson had
almost paid Thornycroft's whole apprenticeship fees
(see indenture on page 8). Nearly a third of the
remaining letters in the Thomas Thornycroft archive
are from Dickenson, easily recognised from the peculiar
habit of making the most of each piece of paper